SIRSHREE

HEAL YOUR DEPRESSION

Be Your Own Counselor

HEAL YOUR DEPRESSION
Be Your Own Counselor

By **Sirshree** Tejparkhi

Copyright © Tejgyan Global Foundation
All Rights Reserved 2024

Tejgyan Global Foundation is a charitable organization
with its headquarters in Pune, India.

ISBN : 978-93-90132-44-7

Published by WOW Publishings Pvt. Ltd., India

First edition published in Apr 2024

Printed and bound by Trinity Academy For Corporate Training Ltd, Pune

This book is based on the Hindi book titled,
"Jeene ki Chaah aur Asha ki Raah" by Sirshree Tejparkhi

Copyright and publishing rights are vested exclusively with WOW Publishings Pvt. Ltd. This book is sold subject to the condition that it shall not by way of trade or otherwise, be lent, resold, hired out, or otherwise circulated without the publisher's prior written consent in any form of binding or cover other than that in which it is published and without a similar condition including this condition being imposed on the subsequent purchaser and without limiting the rights under copyright reserved above, no part of this publication may be reproduced, stored in or introduced into a retrieval system, or transmitted, in any form, or by any means, electronic, mechanical, photocopying, recording or otherwise, without the prior written permission of both the copyright owner and the above-mentioned publisher of this book. Any person who does any unauthorized act in relation to this publication may be liable to criminal prosecution and civil claims for damages.

Although the author and publisher have made every effort to ensure accuracy of content in this book, they hereby disclaim any liability to any party for any loss, damage, or disruption caused by errors or omissions, resulting from negligence, accident, or any other cause. Readers are advised to take full responsibility to exercise discretion in understanding and applying the content of this book.

To,

the compassionate and dedicated bringers of hope,

who work tirelessly to support and guide those

struggling with depression toward recovery and a brighter future.

The never-say-die life-affirmers,

who spark a passion for living within others

and provide guidance toward a fulfilling life.

The vibrant light-bearers,

who seek to breathe new life into the world

and create a reality that transcends all that has been known before.

Thank you for your courage, compassion, and

commitment to making the world a better place.

Disclaimer

The content and techniques presented in this book aim to help individuals dealing with feelings like despondency, mood swings, and disappointment that fall in the category of depression. However, it is important to note that the information provided herein is not intended to address cases of clinical depression that may include psychotic or neurotic symptoms.

Readers are urged to exercise discretion while using this self-help guide when dealing with severe or clinically diagnosed depression. In such cases, it is highly recommended to seek assistance from qualified psychotherapists or mental health professionals for personalized treatment and support.

The author and publisher of this book disclaim any responsibility for the consequences resulting from the exclusive use of the techniques or strategies discussed within for cases of clinical depression. While every effort has been made to ensure the accuracy and effectiveness of the content, readers are encouraged to consult with medical professionals or mental health experts before implementing any advice or recommendations presented in this book.

It is our sincere hope that this book serves as a valuable resource for those seeking to overcome feelings of depression, but we emphasize the importance of seeking appropriate professional help when necessary.

CONTENTS

Disclaimer — 4
Who Should Read This Book? — 7
Preface — 9
How To Benefit From This Book? — 13

PART 1 - INTRODUCTION AND UNDERSTANDING

1. Is It Wrong To Have Depression? — 19
2. Major Causes of Depression — 25
3. More Causes of Depression — 29
4. Stages of Depression — 33

PART 2 - INSIGHTS AND REMEDIES

5. The 3 H Solution — 41
6. Do You Love Yourself? — 46
7. Even This Will Pass Away — 51
8. Outlook and Overlook With Patience — 55
9. It's Just a Matter Of ---- — 61
10. Focusing on Purposeful Actions — 66
11. Harnessing Nature's Healing Power — 70
12. Reclaim Your Inherent Joy and Passion — 75
13. It Doesn't Matter — 80
14. Not a Big Deal — 84

15.	Meditation to Heal the Distress of the Past	88
16.	Living in the Present	90
17.	Bother Then, when 'Then' Becomes Now	94
18.	Steering Clear of Past Hurts	98
19.	Dealing With Emotions	102
20.	The Chain of Thoughts, Feelings, and Mood	107
21.	Understanding Sorrow	111

PART 3 - SPIRITUAL GROWTH AND EMPOWERMENT

22.	The Voice of Faith	117
23.	The Drama of Life	123
24.	Witnessing the Chattering Mind	130
25.	A Meditation to Culminate Our Journey	133

Appendix 1 - Symptoms of Depression	136
Appendix 2 - Guidelines for Caregivers	140
Appendix 3 - Singing Therapy	144
Appendix 4 - Understanding Depression and its Causes: A Statistical Summary	147
Appendix 5 - Revision Chart	155

Who Should Read This Book?

Whether you want to counsel others or equip yourself with practical techniques to navigate life's challenges, this book is for you. It is not just for those grappling with depression or disappointment. It is designed to empower anyone who desires to handle minor and major obstacles that come their way. Join us on a journey of personal growth and development, regardless of your current state of mind.

Here are just a few reasons why it could be exactly what you need:

1. This compelling book imparts a wealth of solutions to help you overcome present life situations, re-kindle and sustain hope for the future. Additionally, you can learn valuable skills to assist others dealing with depression.

2. It is an invaluable resource that can guide you in being a supportive and caring friend or family member to those experiencing depression.

3. Parents will find this book valuable in guiding their children through times of stress or depression. Additionally, it offers comforting guidance to parents who may be dealing with mild depression arising from various challenges related to their health, children, finances, and relationships.

4. If you are interested in counseling others, this book is an inspiring resource that presents a fresh perspective on depression. It

provides insightful questions, practical measures for recovery, and guidance on approaching the problem with kindness, understanding, and a new perspective.

5. This heart-warming book makes a thoughtful gift for anyone struggling with depression. It offers new coping strategies, a deeper understanding of the condition, and a pathway to hope, healing, and happiness.

With stress and anxiety rising in the modern world, this book serves as an essential guide to help in healing depression, whether it is for yourself or for others.

Preface
Are You Ready for a Unique Journey?

The rain had been pouring down for hours as you and your family were returning home from a long vacation. Despite the gloomy weather, everyone was in high spirits, eagerly anticipating the comfort of their beds. As soon as you reached home, the rain stopped, leaving a hot, humid, and overcast atmosphere.

On arriving home, you quickly tried to turn on the air conditioner to combat the hot and humid atmosphere. But when you pressed the button, nothing happened. The lights and fans were still working fine, but the air conditioner remained weirdly silent.

Panic began to set in as you made your way to the living room, frantically attempting to turn on the TV. However, once again, it refused to cooperate. Frustration built up within you, and you began muttering, "Why does this always happen to me? Everything was working fine before we left. Now, suddenly, what happened? How come all the appliances stopped working at once?"

You might not realize it; however, such minor triggers can cause emotional upheavals within a depressed person leading to intense feelings of restlessness, anxiety, and fear in them. In this frame of mind, it is natural to ask, "Why does this always happen to me? Why is the world against me?" The more they dwell on past negative events, the more they feel helpless, victimized, and blamed. The whole world may seem to be against them, and the longer they stay in this mindset, the deeper they sink into depression.

Depression is like a deep, negative impression that is difficult to erase from our minds. Negative experiences leave a profound mark on our lives, and our minds often remember those experiences more readily than positive ones. Harsh words or cruel remarks can leave lasting scars on our psyche that can be challenging to overcome.

In your case, you were upset because the air conditioner and TV were not working. After trying several remedies, such as checking the wiring, turning the main switch off and on, and changing the remote-control batteries, you eventually called your neighbor, who was skilled at fixing electronic devices. Despite his best efforts, he could not fix the problem.

In desperation, you called an electrician who carefully examined the electronic appliances. After cleaning the insides of the remote controls and removing the batteries, the air conditioner and TV suddenly sprang to life. You were astonished that such a minor issue had caused such a major problem. The electrician clarified that moisture had accumulated on the battery contact points due to water spilling from a nearby vase into the remote-control box, making it ineffective.

As you reflected on this incident, you realized that it was merely a minor inconvenience that had been resolved with the prompt help of an expert. In contrast, a person experiencing depression can suffer for years, often reluctant to seek help due to the fear of judgment of what others may think of them. But with the help of a counselor, doctor, insightful book, mentor, or through their own intuition, it is possible to emerge from the abyss of depression.

Each person possesses an inherent power that can be harnessed to heal themselves and others. This book will guide you in discovering and utilizing that power within yourself, empowering you to become a counselor.

Depression is not a disease but rather a framework of negative feelings and thoughts. Every individual experiencing depression has the potential to heal themselves. With the help of honest self-reflection and self-talk, they can break free of negative emotions and thoughts. Just as one must clearly explain the symptoms to a doctor to seek proper treatment for an illness, individuals grappling with depression must be honest with themselves about their feelings and thoughts. Only then will they be able to heal themselves.

Self-counseling is a healing journey in which we observe our way of working and our mind's excuses, tendencies, fixations, beliefs, and thoughts. Sometimes, the mind creates excuses, avoids facing the situation, or becomes emotionally weak during this process. In these situations, three main qualities—patience, faith, and self-motivation—are required to persevere in this journey. If we can adhere to these three qualities, our journey will only culminate in growth.

Furthermore, we need to understand what depression is. What are the various types of depression? How can one identify if they are suffering from depression? Is every unhappy person necessarily depressed? Is there a permanent cure? This book addresses answers to all these questions.

Remember, when someone is hungry, simply being served food is not enough; they must also eat it. Similarly, if we do not put what we learn into practice, then it is not possible heal depression.

In this journey, it is essential to grasp the understanding and practice self-counseling to promote healing for yourself and also for others. This will be accomplished by walking on the path of hope.

Congratulations on embarking on this journey. You have read this book so far, which means there is someone within you, who wants to be healed. Wish you success in this endeavor!

How To Benefit From This Book?

Have you ever stood before a mirror and engaged in a heartfelt conversation with yourself as if you were conversing with a friend?

Have you ever shared your innermost feelings with a beloved pet or an inanimate object and poured out your deepest emotions?

Surprising as it may sound, pets or objects can profoundly sense your feelings even though they cannot respond or comprehend. After speaking to them, you may feel content within.

Expressing our feelings verbally or in written form has been proven to alleviate stress. Whether we speak into a mirror, to a toy, a favorite object, a pet, or a plant, the medium is not as significant as the relief it brings.

At some point in life, everyone experiences disappointment, sadness, or heartbreak and wishes, "If only I had a friend I could trust, someone who I could confide in about the pain in my heart and express my feelings freely." Those who cannot find someone to confide in often endure a life of stress, despair, and emotional suffocation. By continuously suppressing their emotions, they may eventually become victims of depression.

In response to this predicament, psychotherapy clinics and counseling centers have been established in many places so people can visit them to alleviate their mental burden. Hotlines and text message services are available for essential support at some locations. While some of these services may come at a cost, they offer some solace to troubled minds.

However, there may be some issues that most people would feel hesitant or embarrassed to discuss with the counselors openly.

To address this problem, this book is being presented as a 24/7 counselor. Whether you take help from this counselor for yourself or for counseling others, answering all the questions in this book can provide relief. Needless to say, this counseling service will be completely free of cost.

The book is structured as a series of counseling sessions. To derive the full benefit from this book, you need to adhere to the following instructions, which are categorized into three parts.

1. Instructions to be followed before reading the session

   a) Ensure you sit with a notepad, pencil, or pen. For optimal results, it is recommended to read only one session per day.

   b) Sit with a mirror, a favorite object, or a pet.

   c) If you prefer, close the door of your room to maintain privacy and ensure your voice is not heard outside.

   d) Be mentally prepared to take notes on what the counselor—in this case, the session in the book—tells you.

   e) Some statements may assume your answer is "Yes." If your answer or response differs, please ignore it for the time being and continue reading. You will find answers to your specific questions as you progress.

2. Instructions to be followed during the session

While reading this session, you will notice different symbols that require specific actions. You should pause your reading and follow these specific instructions associated with each symbol.

a) **Dialog box:**

You will be asked to answer some questions and share your thoughts. Imagine you are speaking to someone face to face as you respond. Feel free to choose to talk to a mirror, your favorite object, or your pet as your confidante. Since no one is physically present, you can express yourself openly without any hesitation while discussing any personal matter.

b) **Writing box:**

When you come across this symbol, set the book aside and begin writing. Resume reading only after you have finished writing. You can take notes in a diary, notepad, or even on your mobile phone.

c) **Contemplation box:**

Whenever you see this symbol, close your eyes, and contemplate. Think about the given scenario or question from various angles and perspectives, and how it applies to your situation.

d) **Action box:**

Occasionally, you will be asked to perform certain activities while reading. Set the book aside and complete that activity before continuing to read.

3. Instructions to be followed after reading the session

After completing each chapter, you must work on an action plan until the next session. For example, you may decide to repeat self-affirmations that are provided in some sessions. These magical statements can serve as a powerful tool to help you get better results.

It is essential to remember these instructions while reading the book to gain maximum benefit from its content.

The book is divided into three parts:

Part 1: Introduction and Understanding

In this part, you will find an introduction to what depression is, its causes, and the stages of its onset.

Part 2: Insights and Remedies

In this part, you will discover simple yet powerful methods that will assist you in learning the art of perceiving depression from a new standpoint. Although these techniques may appear straightforward, their power lies in their simplicity. Upon introspection, they can yield excellent results that can ignite a profound desire within you to lead a happy life.

Part 3: Spiritual Growth and Empowerment

The third part delves into advanced techniques designed to elevate your spiritual quotient and enhance your physical and mental capabilities. It unearths new aspects that can spark an unfailing hope, empowering you to become an effective counselor for yourself and others. Through this process, you will lead a life free from despair.

By diligently practicing the instructions outlined in this book, you will not only uplift yourself but also counsel others to rise above the quagmire of despair. So, without further ado, let us embark on this path of hope with the auspicious desire to lead a vibrant and purposeful life. May your journey be filled with hope and fulfillment.

PART 1

INTRODUCTION AND UNDERSTANDING

1

Is It Wrong To Have Depression?

Welcome to your first counseling session. Today marks the beginning of a new chapter of your life. As you reflect on your journey thus far, you may recall encountering numerous crossroads and challenges that left you feeling confused and overwhelmed. Amidst the emotional roller-coaster of joy and sorrow, you have learned how to move forward and progress.

Now, as you leave the past behind, are you ready to take control of your life and steer it on a new, smoother path? If so, congratulations on garnering the strength to work on yourself. In these self-counseling sessions, you will discover the tools needed to achieve healing from depression and initiate a new start.

You might be wondering, what exactly is depression?

In recent times, people of all ages, from children to the aged, claim to have experienced depression. According to the World Health Organization (WHO), one in five people has experienced depression. With the emergence of Covid-19, the pandemic has been identified as one of the leading causes of depression in recent times.

While depression has become a commonly used term, what does it indeed mean? Is it a treatable condition? How does it differ from sadness or disappointment? How can we distinguish between them?

Unfortunately, there is no physical test for depression; it is diagnosed clinically. Several psychological and social factors can contribute to depression, such as genetics, trauma, low self-esteem, biochemical changes, pressure to excel, emotional issues, social and environmental factors like exposure to violence, neglect, abuse, or poverty.

Typical symptoms of depression include a persistent low mood, loss of interest in activities once enjoyed, fluctuations in weight and appetite, irregular sleep, fatigue, slower movements and speech, feelings of worthlessness or guilt, and negative or suicidal thoughts.

It is common for some people to confuse disappointment with depression. Let's explore the difference through an example.

Imagine a girl who had meticulously planned her future. After graduating from college with high hopes and dreams, she enthusiastically applied for numerous positions in various organizations but faced rejection from each one. With each rejection, her initial enthusiasm gave way to sadness, as she started to believe that she must be lacking in some way, which led to constant setbacks. As rejections continued to pile up, her frustration intensified, eventually leading her into a state of depression.

Anxiety is another emotional state that is occasionally mistaken for depression. Anxiety is a common and normal human emotion that everyone experiences at some point in their life. When someone is anxious, they may feel fear and restlessness or have panic or anxiety disorders. It is often a result of prolonged stress. While anxiety and depression can share some overlapping symptoms, they are distinct conditions.

It is natural to experience fear, anxiety, anger, and stress, as these were the coping mechanisms that our ancestors developed as hunters and gatherers in prehistoric times. The human brain developed these programmed reactions as a fight-or-flight mechanism when faced with danger. However, with the evolution of civilized society, man has become a social being. The pressures we face today are often less about physical danger and more about fitting into a societal framework and achieving socially recognized success. This shift means that even the most trivial of interactions in our daily lives can evoke intense emotional responses, highlighting the intricate relationship between our primal instincts and the demands of modern life.

Thus, feelings of sadness, sorrow, anxiety, and disappointment have become commonplace in civilized human life. However, if they persist for an extended period, they can lead to depression. It is crucial to recognize the differences between typical emotional reactions and depression. Just because someone faces problems, sadness, disappointment, or anxiety for some time, it does not necessarily mean they have depression, as these are all normal human emotions. When these emotional states are handled promptly, depression can undoubtedly be prevented.

The most important thing to understand is that encountering failure is perfectly normal when striving for something significant in life. However, it is essential to have faith that nature is continually working to fulfill our wishes in accordance with our prayers.

While nature may take its time to resolve our problems, our mind often anticipates immediate results. When we face obstacles or experience delays in fulfilling our desires, we may feel helpless, sad, and disappointed. However, if we elevate our understanding that nature has its timeline and it is perfectly normal to face delays, we can prevent inviting depression into our lives.

Let's revisit the example of the girl mentioned earlier. Nature is searching for the place where the girl can make the most significant impact on a global scale. Perhaps she was not meant to work for those organizations, or they were not the right fit for her. She may continue to face rejection until she finds her rightful place. This is a beautiful arrangement made by nature.

Feeling incredibly sad when facing rejection is normal. However, understanding that nature has its own timeline can prevent disappointment. So, the next time you face rejection while seeking a job or marriage alliance, or go through a breakup, remind yourself,

"It is perfectly normal! I am one step closer to finding what's truly best for me!" This clarity can significantly reduce your grief and prevent you from becoming depressed.

The lessons learned during these challenging times will be a significant achievement in your life. As you focus on them, the challenging times will pass, leading you to discover a new way of living.

 Recall a situation in which you feel whatever is happening to you is common in everyone's life and is perfectly normal.

Is there any incident in your life that you feel is not normal?
☐ Yes / ☐ No

Even if your answer is "Yes," there is no need to worry. The mind often struggles to accept that a situation we find personal and unique to us is actually quite normal and common. Consider, for instance, the loss of a loved one. It is a kind of grief that rocks our world and may lead us down a tunnel of depression, but it is normal, and with time, we accept it as so. By reframing the situation and accepting its normalcy, we can learn to cope with the challenging circumstances in a healthy way and move toward healing.

Know for sure that whatever you are feeling is perfectly fine. Do not label yourself or get overwhelmed by your feelings. Simply, being aware of your thoughts and feelings is the first step, and you have the power to understand and do something about it. The mind often refuses to acknowledge that a situation you are struggling to cope with is normal.

If the mind continues to falter, one way to trick the mind is to make the situation humorous. This approach does not mean that we are undermining the situation; rather, it allows the mind to pause and consider the incident from a unique perspective, effectively rewiring the thought processes in our brains.

So, how can you inject humor into a difficult situation? Think about how you sometimes use the fast-forward button to skip scenes in a movie or a show. When you watch an action scene or a tragic song in fast-forward mode, it looks comical and makes you burst into laughter. Similarly, you can apply the same trick to the things that make you feel depressed.

Now, recall a sad incident and visualize it in fast-forward mode, like a comedy scene. Imagine what will happen when you visualize it like a comic scene. Listen to the dialogues from that incident by using the voices of Walt Disney characters like Mickey Mouse or Donald Duck. You will laugh. The previously overwhelming situation begins to appear comparatively trivial and manageable. You can then approach it with a lighter mood. Repeatedly recalling that incident 2 to 3 times will reduce its impact on you. Eventually, it will seem normal or will no longer elicit the same level of sadness.

Now, recall a sad but trivial experience of your choice, and let us walk through some tips on transforming it into a comical scene.

1. Imagine the incident as a black-and-white clip with funny interruptions.
2. Listen to it in cartoon language or voice.
3. Watch it in dim, dull light.
4. Picture the incident as a painting or a piece of art.
5. Visualize the incident disintegrating into small sand particles as you walk through it.
6. Further, visualize the sand particles dissolving in space as you revisit it.

How do you feel after this exercise?

Does the incident still disturb you as much, or has its intensity reduced?
☐ Yes / ☐ No / ☐ Other

Following this session, adopt a fresh outlook when facing similar sad incidents by viewing them as comical scenes in either fast-forward or slow-motion mode. Creatively experiment with various approaches until our next session. Thank you!

2

Major Causes of Depression

Hello, how are you doing?

 Before we begin our discussion today, can you think of the possible causes of depression? Please write them down.

You may have written down some causes of depression. Now, we will learn about the three main causes of depression.

1. Situations

Every day, we encounter various situations that shake us. Some minor ones can be quickly forgotten within a few hours, allowing us to carry on with our everyday routines. However, some situations are so significant that we take a few days or even months to recover from them. These situations leave such a deep impact on us that it seems nearly impossible to move past them. They embed themselves so deeply in our memory that constantly recalling them makes us susceptible to physical and mental illnesses.

Sometimes, during our daily activities, we may feel disappointed when things don't unfold as anticipated. When we put in a lot of effort and the outcome is unfavorable, or when we don't receive much appreciation, we can feel disheartened and dejected. At times, it may feel as if we have become depressed. However, this is a common state of the mind, which is nowadays labeled as "depression."

In today's world, the term "depression" is commonly used to describe even the slightest setback. When someone says, "You look depressed," we might feel scared and perceive it as an incurable disease, leading to even more despair. However, every problem has a solution. Whenever a problem arises, there is always an underlying cause and where there is a cause, there is also a way to overcome it. Yet, due to fear, we find ourselves disregarding both the cause and the potential remedy to the problem.

If you believe that you may be experiencing depression, take a moment to reflect on your past and try to identify when it began. Did you go through any unpleasant situation that still lingers in your mind? Or did you convince yourself, based on someone's hearsay, that you are depressed?

 Recall and write down the incident or cause that could have triggered your depression.

It is crucial to write because writing allows us to discover the causes, and once we identify the causes, we can treat ourselves in a timely manner.

2. Social reasons

The occurrence of depression was almost negligible a few generations ago. But it is on the rise lately. Nowadays, people have undergone significant changes in their lifestyles, with nuclear families becoming the norm. Additionally, increased aspirations, the allure of material possessions, peer pressure, and intense competition have collectively fueled the prevalence of depression.

Due to social conditioning, people believe that they must conform to certain norms to gain social acceptance. They fear their life will be deemed worthless if they don't meet these expectations. For instance, they feel pressurized to get married by a certain age, have a girlfriend or a boyfriend by a certain age, build a career that enables them to buy a car and a house, and so on.

Some people experience depression triggered by thoughts such as, "What will happen now? What will people say?" when they reach a certain age without marrying or having children. Others face challenges like job losses, business setbacks, relationship breakups, children's struggles, exploitation, defamation, and various other social and familial pressures. These pressures can contribute to feelings of depression.

 What social or familial pressure are you facing today?

3. Loneliness

Many people harbor deep concerns about their social image and work tirelessly to maintain it, sometimes at the cost of their well-being. They often isolate themselves to protect their false image and prevent discord in relationships, resulting in withdrawal from social interactions. With the fear of judgment or exposure of their true thoughts, which could damage their social image, they end up feeling lonely and depressed. Many others suffer from loneliness that comes as a result of their life circumstances such as loss of loves ones. Indeed, loneliness is a significant cause of depression.

Social media aggravates this issue by offering a constant stream of entertainment that captivates both young and old, often leading to hours of engagement. However, the allure of the online world can cause people to lose sight of their true selves and become disconnected from their genuine identity. To escape boredom, many people try to present themselves as more appealing or superior to others on social media, forgetting that it is merely a form of entertainment. When the façade eventually crumbles, it can leave them feeling lonely, disillusioned, and depressed. Ironically, the rise of social media may be a driving force for loneliness in some.

While there are many causes of depression, our outlook on life ultimately determines whether a situation becomes a stepping stone for growth or plunges us into an abyss of depression. Everyone's nature is different, as is their perspective on situations.

For instance, when two youths fail in a job interview, one of them might think, "This is it; I'm finished. Why couldn't I perform better? How will I make ends meet? I can never be successful." This negative mindset leads them to despair.

On the other hand, the second one might think, "Perhaps the person who got this job needed it more than I did. This is the will of God. I just need to keep trying. Nature has something better in store for me, which will soon unfold. The best job meant for me will come my way soon." This positive way of thinking can eventually lead them to success.

In certain instances, changing the situation or its outcome may not be within our control. Nonetheless, we can always choose to approach it with a positive outlook to avoid disappointment and distress.

In the next session, we will explore more causes of depression. Before that, take a moment to reflect on any situations that come to your mind and write them down. Thank you.

3

More Causes of Depression

Let's start today's session with an insightful story. In a village, a boatman used to ferry people across the river. He was a good-hearted man, but he had a tendency to worry about trivial matters. One fine morning, as he was about to begin his usual routine, he noticed a tiny hole in his boat through which water had begun seeping in. This sight worried him, and he started thinking, "What if the hole doesn't get fixed? How will I make a living? How will I manage the household and my children's education? Today, there is a fair on the other side of the river, and I could have made more money, but what now?"

The boatman was so engrossed in these thoughts that even after several passengers boarded his boat, he continued rowing forward while being preoccupied with worries about his livelihood. Consequently, when the boat reached a distance, it began to get flooded with water, causing panic among the passengers. Although everyone was eventually rescued, the passengers lost faith in the boatman.

 What do you learn from this story?

You may think the boatman was foolish for not plugging the leakage first, which seems like common sense. Perhaps this thought occurred to the boatman as well. But he was so overwhelmed by worries that he could not work out a plan and act on it.

When faced with a minor problem, people often ruminate over it day and night. Due to their excessive negative thinking, they become overwhelmed by their fears, worries, and apprehensions, which can lead to inaction. Excessive negative thinking and inaction are some of the causes of depression.

 Take a moment to reflect on which subject or issue you tend to overthink and jot it down.

Some people often engage in overthinking, which is typically associated with a negative mindset. In this state, they tend to focus on faults or shortcomings, leaving little room for optimism.

Consider a situation where a person is stuck in traffic. A person with a negative mindset might say, "This is terrible. I am going to be late. This traffic is never going to clear up. Why does this always happen to me?"

Meanwhile, a person with a positive mindset might say, "I can use this time to catch up on my audiobook or podcast. I am grateful for the chance to slow down and take a break from my busy day. Maybe there is a good reason for this delay that I don't yet understand."

Someone who wants to think positively can even appreciate a nonfunctional clock for showing the right time at least twice a day! They will try to find positivity in everything.

Indeed, overthinking itself is not the problem. The problem arises when there is a lack of clarity in our thinking. We have not been taught how to perceive events with optimism. When we try to solve a situation with a negative perspective, it becomes even more complicated. Therefore, we need to deliberately guide our thinking in the right direction and start seeing the positive in negative situations, objects, and people. This will lend a new direction to our thinking.

 Now, intentionally try to find and describe three positive things from an adverse event in your life.

Great! Now, let's understand the next cause of depression, which involves changes happening in the body due to disease, hormonal imbalance, or genetics.

Severe or chronic illnesses can significantly impact one's physical and emotional well-being, limiting their ability to function. You may have observed that when someone depends on others due to their illness, they struggle to accept it. Coping with dependence on others can be a challenging experience, often leading to irritability, frustration, and disinterest. The affected individuals may feel they are being a burden on their loved ones and experience a sense of guilt or hopelessness, which can lead to depression.

Children with physical disabilities may feel disheartened when taunted or ridiculed by others. Their parents may also experience despair, worrying about their future and struggling to determine the best ways to support them. Coping with physical disabilities can be a long, arduous, challenging journey, often requiring significant adjustments in daily life.

 Can you share any experiences with a chronic or persistent disease you or an acquaintance has faced in the past two years?

Do they currently experience any mental stress related to that illness?

☐ Yes / ☐ No

This question is being posed because the mere thought of illness can make one mentally weak, leading to depression.

Consider a man who was informed he had cancer after undergoing a blood test. His world turned upside down, and he began worrying about his survival and his family's welfare after his death. His constant engagement in anxious thoughts about his situation affected his emotional and physical well-being. He stopped eating and had emotional breakdowns. Once, when he broke down in tears, his friend inquired about the reason behind his distress.

Thankfully, his friend took him to another doctor, who questioned the initial report and ordered a re-examination. The new report showed that everything was normal and revealed a typing mistake which had led to the man's name appearing on someone else's report.

This instance highlights how over-worrying without clarity can adversely affect physical and mental health.

Have you witnessed someone experience similar circumstances, or has this happened to you? ☐ Yes / ☐ No

Besides illnesses, an imbalance in various neurotransmitters and enzymes also contributes to anxiety and depression.

Teenagers find it difficult to come to terms with the changes happening in their bodies during adolescence. These hormonal changes are a normal part of development. However, in some cultures, children are not provided proper guidance or support on this subject, either in schools or by family members, due to social taboos. As a result, they perceive these changes as an abnormality. This leads to an unsettling curiosity, stress, and unnecessary peer pressure due to a lack of understanding and direction. This can make them feel disheartened and lost in their situation.

Besides this, various chemicals produced in our nervous system play a significant role in influencing our emotions. Imbalances in chemicals like dopamine, serotonin, adrenaline, cortisol, and norepinephrine, contribute to feelings of disappointment and hopelessness that can aggravate depression.

Throughout life, we face various challenges that can be both physically and mentally taxing. Our mindset and how we approach these challenges can significantly affect our emotional and mental well-being. If we approach these situations with a clear and open mind, we can prevent feelings of lethargy and sadness from turning into depression. Viewing even the worst situation optimistically can create a placebo-positive change. Accepting our situations and emotions as an integral facet of life can help us cope better and live more fulfilling lives.

4

Stages of Depression

Welcome to today's session. In the previous session, we explored various causes of depression and understood the importance of deliberately choosing to find the positive aspects in every situation.

In today's session, let's understand the different stages through which depression sets in. This understanding is vital because prevention is more effective than trying to climb out of deep depression. We have the power to redirect our lives with a little awareness, but if we allow negative thoughts to entangle us, we invite despair. When we nip the habit in the bud, it won't become a full-blown tendency, but once it takes hold, breaking free becomes significantly more challenging. Similarly, identifying subtle negative feelings early can prevent them from spiraling out of control.

Let's explore how the mind gradually leads us into depression and at which stage we need to be more vigilant.

1. Non-acceptance of situations and unfulfillment of expectations

When faced with an undesirable incident, the mind often struggles to accept it. It might react, "This can't be right; this can't be happening," or "This is wrong news."

Consider someone who had recently met a close friend or loved one. If they come to know about their sudden demise, they just cannot accept their death and plunge into deep shock.

Similarly, in the pursuit of more comforts and luxury, someone purchases a house, a car, and various other appliances on credit. However, they suddenly lose their job and are confronted with unexpected medical bills for a family member. When they start facing a financial crisis, they cannot accept the harsh reality and begin to feel disappointed.

When our expectations remain unfulfilled or when we encounter situations that test our ability to accept them, it can trigger a cascade of negative thoughts and emotions. These emotions may encompass disappointment, frustration, anger, and sorrow and can even aggravate to feelings of hopelessness, helplessness, and despair. The longer we persist in this emotional turmoil, the more intense and pervasive these negative feelings can become, ultimately resulting in apathy and aloofness from the world around us.

At the core of this issue lies the disparity between our expectations and the reality we face, which originates from our inability to accept what is. When these two aspects do not align, we may experience disillusionment, a sense of being cheated or betrayed, and even question our beliefs, values, and our very identity. This can further erode our self-confidence and self-esteem, making it even more challenging to cope with the inevitable challenges and setbacks that life presents.

It is natural to encounter situations that we find difficult to accept, and our minds may develop defense mechanisms, such as repressing or ignoring such experiences, to shield us from these harsh realities. However, these coping mechanisms can potentially lead to specific disorders.

Take a moment to reflect on an experience in your life that you still struggle to accept today and write about it below. It is okay if you still find it hard to accept, but addressing these challenges can be the first step toward finding peace and healing.

By becoming more self-aware, we can identify negative situations as they arise in our lives. Learning to accept these situations, rather than resisting or denying them, is a significant step. In this context, acceptance doesn't imply that we must like or agree with these situations; rather, it means acknowledging their existence, accepting the way we feel about them, and working toward resolution. When we can genuinely accept negative situations early on, we can prevent ourselves from sinking deeper into depression. The longer we resist or deny these circumstances, the more negative thoughts and emotions can take hold, pushing us further down the path of despair.

Acceptance is not an easy task and necessitates a certain level of emotional maturity and resilience. Nevertheless, it is a crucial step in maintaining mental health and overall well-being. Through practice, we can learn to cultivate greater acceptance of negative situations and gain control over our reactions rather than allowing these situations to dictate our emotional state.

2. Anger

Anger often erupts when we encounter resistance to a situation. Sometimes, this anger may arise seemingly without any apparent reason, leading to persistent irritation. In such a situation, no matter how much one might try to appear calm on the surface, a storm of thoughts continues to rage in their mind.

For instance, as seen in the earlier example, when someone faces a shortage of money, they become overwhelmed with numerous negative thoughts. They may think, "How will I overcome this problem? My dreams seem like burden now. Why did I buy such a large house? How will I manage finances in the future?" Such thoughts can be highly irritating and may result in occasional outbursts of anger over trivial matters.

When people are consumed by rage, they often lash out at others. While this may provide them temporary relief, it can lead to others distancing them, ultimately leaving them feeling isolated. If they had remained calm in those situations, they could have sought compassion and cooperation from others and managed to cope with the depression. It is wise to steer clear of anger in depression; otherwise, situations can deteriorate to such an extent that they become difficult to control.

Reflect on times when you experience anger. Is anger typically linked to non-acceptance of circumstances?

3. Guilt

Over time, frequent expressions of anger in different situations can trigger feelings of guilt within an individual.

For instance, in the earlier example, when the person continually expresses anger, their family members might hold them accountable for the situation and blame, "Why did you buy such a large house on a mortgage? We had already advised you that there is no need for such a big house. But you never listen to anyone; you act on your whims. Now, suffer the consequences." Hearing this repeatedly, the person also starts assuming responsibility for the situation and begins to live in guilt.

In the third stage, one may turn to God, Allah, or a higher divine power to seek forgiveness for the mistakes or choices that led to their current situation, or they may consider themselves responsible for it. They may yearn to break free from the situation but feel helpless and unable to make improvements.

Remaining vigilant and self-aware at this stage can lead to intensified prayers, which can ultimately contribute to their liberation from depression.

4. Addiction and blaming others

When one is plagued with guilt, their mind is in a constant state of unrest. To escape the incessant negative thoughts and seek solace, they may resort to various forms of addiction, such as alcohol, smoking, excessive TV or cell phone use, overeating, or oversleeping. However, these activities offer only temporary relief from their inner turmoil.

In this state, they blame others for their situation because deep down, they hesitate to take responsibility for their situation and also find it difficult to face the situation. They develop a victim mindset and become habitual in seeking sympathy from their family members by expressing helplessness. This behavior can become a kind of addiction in itself, as it makes them constantly seek support or validation from others.

Those who frequently exhibit anger, shift blame onto others for their problems, or become overly reliant on others, often find themselves avoided by those around them.

It is crucial to reflect on whether we hold ourselves accountable for our circumstances or tend to shift the blame onto others. This self-examination is pivotal in breaking free from the cycle of guilt and addiction.

 Do you consider yourself responsible for your current situation, or do you tend to blame someone else for it?

5. Becoming unsociable

As depression advances, individuals may develop an increasing fear of engaging with others, especially in group settings. This fear can lead to social anxiety, making them feel uncomfortable and self-conscious in the company of others. They may encounter unexplained anxieties that leave them feeling overwhelmed and trapped, further reinforcing their inclination to avoid social situations, leading to disinterest in socializing and distancing themselves from others.

This growing unsociability can result in increased self-isolation, with individuals preferring to keep their feelings and thoughts to themselves. This breakdown in communication can make them feel withdrawn from social interactions and challenged to express their needs or seek support from friends and family.

6. Extreme depression

Extreme depression is a complex mental health disorder that can manifest in various forms. The final stage of depression, often referred to as deep depression or major depressive disorder, is typically the most severe and debilitating. Individuals in this stage often experience overwhelming sadness, hopelessness, and despair. Finding joy or pleasure in activities they once enjoyed becomes challenging, and they may struggle to maintain their regular daily activities, such as work, school, or social interactions.

In addition to emotional and behavioral symptoms, deep depression can also manifest physically. Individuals may undergo significant changes in appetite and weight, experience sleep disturbances such as insomnia or excessive sleeping, and feel fatigued or suffer from an immense loss of energy. They may also have difficulty concentrating or making decisions and may experience feelings of worthlessness or guilt.

The severity of these symptoms can potentially lead to self-harm and even suicidal thoughts, underscoring the importance of individuals experiencing these symptoms seeking help from a mental health professional, such as a psychiatrist or psychologist. These professionals can offer therapy, medication, or a combination of approaches to assist individuals in managing their symptoms and regaining control and stability in their lives.

Without proper treatment, individuals may become resigned to their condition and give up on efforts to recover. It is crucial to recognize the signs of deep depression and seek professional help as soon as possible to prevent the exacerbation of symptoms and potential harm to themselves.

The purpose of providing information about these stages of depression is to raise awareness and encourage individuals to urgently seek counseling and support to aid in their recovery. It is essential to remember that deep depression is a treatable condition. With proper assistance and a positive mindset, individuals can regain control over their lives and work toward a brighter future.

With this session, we have reached the end of Part 1 of the book. Part 2 of the book presents profound insights and effective remedies to overcome depression.

PART 2

INSIGHTS AND REMEDIES

5

The 3 H Solution

 Take a moment to jog your memory and narrate what you recall from Part 1 of the book.

Sad feelings or disappointment should not be labeled as depression. They are normal emotions that everyone experiences at some point in their life. Instead of dwelling on them, we should view them as opportunities to evolve and make our lives more easygoing and manageable. However, if we allow ourselves to linger in these feelings of sadness, we run the risk of letting depression take hold to such an extent that we may even lose our desire to live.

How is your current state? What is your level of disappointment at present?

☐ Too little / ☐ Little / ☐ High / ☐ Very high

Do you sense a decline in your desire to live?

☐ Yes / ☐ No / ☐ Sometimes / ☐ Other

When people are sad and frustrated, their enthusiasm for life often fades away. They may stop loving themselves and start viewing themselves as worthless, negative, and lethargic. This can negatively affect their life energy.

Life energy or vitality is an invaluable gift bestowed upon us by nature. Regrettably, many of us fail to recognize its value and allow even the slightest disappointment or problem to bring sadness, quickly diminishing our desire to live. As a result, our life energy begins to wane, making our bodies more vulnerable to ailments.

Consider the case of a young woman who aspired to be a professional dancer. Unfortunately, she suffered a severe injury in a road accident due to which her leg had to be amputated, compelling her to stop dancing and shattering her dream. This news proved to be devastating, leaving her feeling hopeless and defeated.

If she could sustain her will to live, she would find ways to cope with the injury and work toward recovery. She developed resilience by reading inspiring biographies of people who faced similar situations yet overcame them and achieved remarkable feats. Drawing inspiration from these individuals and committing to the exercises prescribed by her doctor, she boosted her life energy and improved her chances of regaining the ability to dance. With a positive and understanding attitude, she found the strength to overcome the cloud of depression and bounce back with renewed passion and purpose. She is none other than the renowned Indian classical dancer Sudha Chandran, who serves as an inspiration to countless people looking for that ray of hope.

It is essential to have patience and take things one step at a time, as the journey to recovery can be challenging. However, if one's desire to live decreases, they may resort to unhealthy habits such as overeating or consuming junk food to escape frustration. Indulging in a bar of chocolate may briefly alleviate their sadness and temporarily boost their energy and relief. Still, it is vital to recognize that these habits are unsustainable and can lead to further complications.

A depressed person may inadvertently develop various forms of addiction as a means to escape disappointment. They may overeat, spend excessive hours on their cell phone or watching TV, and resort to oversleeping, heavy smoking, or alcohol consumption. These choices indicate a gradual decline in their desire and will to live, and the consequences of these decisions are evident in their diminished quality of life.

While not everyone who exhibits these behaviors is necessarily depressed, those suffering from depression are more likely to experience them.

 Consider examining your lifestyle for any similar habits.

A person interested in boosting their life energy will keep away from addictions. By practicing self-love, they release unnecessary worries and channel their life energy toward positive endeavors. As they pursue loftier goals, they use depression as a springboard to rise higher, gaining mastery over their body and mind. Their life energy and willpower surge, empowering them to conquer any illness, anxiety, or crisis.

Life energy is a precious gift that can be nurtured and amplified by making positive choices every day. Those who choose to do so will undoubtedly reap the rewards of a fulfilling and meaningful life.

Let us understand the 3 H's that can boost your vitality and guide you toward new goals.

1. <u>Heal</u> with self-love and self-respect

Take a moment for honest introspection: "What actions do I take to seek attention and respect from others? How do I express anger in the hope of getting people to agree with me? How do I display arrogance to gain attention from others? And when these efforts go unnoticed, how does it affect my feelings of hurt and unhappiness?"

Through conscious reflection, we realize that we often depend on others for our happiness. We tend to believe that our happiness is contingent upon receiving others' attention, respect, approval, and love.

To overcome this dependency, we must learn to respect and accept ourselves just as we are. Instead of constantly seeking attention, respect, and approval from others, we should focus on ourselves.

Self-love means respecting ourselves and being responsible for our own happiness. It is not about giving in to harmful habits or addictions to satisfy our desires, but about finding joy in being independent from external dependencies.

When we love and respect ourselves, our emotional wounds start to heal. By relying on ourselves for happiness and taking responsibility for it, we create little room for sorrow. Self-love brings positivity to our thoughts and feelings; it acts as a healing balm, not only for ourselves but also for those around us.

2. Cultivating the <u>habit</u> of recalling positive events

We must develop the habit of remembering the positive events in our lives, especially when negative thoughts arise in our minds.

For example, if you find yourself sitting in a relaxed state and suddenly an old memory, fear, or worry resurfaces, tell yourself, "Alright, this negative thought has surfaced. Now, let me recollect a positive event from my life."

Recall the best moments that have occurred this year or the year before. Remember the problems you successfully solved, the crises you confidently overcame, or the favorite places you have visited.

By cultivating this habit, we nurture a state of happiness and well-being. Once this habit is developed, consider the session successful.

 Now, narrate three outstanding events that have happened in your life in the last three years.

3. <u>Harbor</u> knowledge that has the potential to inspire you

In this step, you need to acquire knowledge that will encourage and inspire you to declare, **"I can do anything."**

Make it a habit to read the biographies of great individuals who, despite facing failures, remained undeterred and achieved success. Reading about them will boost your morale and ignite a desire to achieve what you want.

When we marvel at the arrangements nature has made, from ants to elephants, we feel motivated. We have been witnessing such wonders since our childhood. However, when we stopped appreciating them and took the gifts of nature for granted, sadness began to seep in. When we stopped loving and respecting ourselves, we became overwhelmed with sorrow.

Now, we must learn to rediscover the childlike wonder and amazement we once had for the world around us. We must consciously love and respect ourselves, soaking in the beauty and marvels of nature and the world. This will help us experience the joy of freedom from sorrow.

Invest some time to contemplate the insights gained from this session. See you in the next session. Till then, take care and love yourself as you are. Thank you.

6

Do You Love Yourself?

"Your life is invaluable to your family. You radiate love from within. Your presence fills the hearts of those around you with love. You embody immense purity. You always shower others with love; in return, others love you, too."

Upon hearing these words, you might wonder, "Who are these words being said for?" These words are being said for you. They are meant for you, the one who is reading and conversing through the medium of this book.

You may feel disillusioned and say, "Wouldn't that be nice? It seems like no one genuinely loves me. Everyone in this world appears selfish, driven by their own selfish motives. They all seem to pretend to love as long as it serves their purpose, but once their ulterior motive is fulfilled, they don't even bother to inquire about others. Instead, they callously abandon them."

"Alright! Do your parents and siblings love you?"

Regardless of your response, if you look deep within, the answer will often be a resounding "Yes."

You may say, "Familial love doesn't count, as they are blood relations connected to me by default, while other relatives are selfish. Expecting any form of genuine love from them is futile."

So, tell me, "Who are those people who don't love you?" Take a moment to ponder on this question.

"While several people could be on your list, is your name on that list? Do you truly love yourself?"

If the answer is "Yes," it does not matter whether others love you. When you do not expect love from others, you spare yourself from the anguish of disappointment, the sorrow of longing, and the torment of worry. The belief that "No one loves me, no one likes me" leads you to perceive yourself as unworthy.

God has created every human being perfectly. However, often, it is the cruel grip of societal ignorance and the relentless barrage of criticism received from one's own family members that can leave one shattered and dejected. Many start perceiving themselves as insignificant, worthless, unvalued, and incompetent. They begin to disregard their own inherent virtues, forgetting to embrace self-love. It is a tragic tale akin to a majestic flower being crushed under an unforgiving force.

Let's understand how Nicholas or Nick Vujicic overcame this situation. Nick Vujicic, an Australian motivational speaker and the president of the non-profit organization "Life Without Limbs," was born in 1982 in Melbourne, Australia, without limbs. Doctors could not explain his deformity and his birth was considered a tragedy. He suffered from tetra amelia syndrome, and his childhood was plagued by bullying, teasing, depression, and loneliness.

He constantly questioned why he was different from all the other kids surrounding him and why he was the one born without arms and legs. He wondered what the purpose of his life was or if he even had a purpose. It was not until there was a complete U-turn in his life that things began to change. His mother read him an article from the newspaper about a man who continued to be happy despite being disabled, and that's when Nick had an "Aha" moment! He realized that life without limbs does not mean a life without purpose.

At the age of 17, Nick started giving motivational speeches in his prayer group, eventually leading him to become a motivational speaker and a positive change-maker in other people's lives. Later, he founded two organizations: a non-profit organization and ministry called "Life Without Limbs" and another one called "Attitude is Altitude," with the aim of sharing stories of good faith and positive change with everyone. Nick has also authored several books, including "Life Without Limits: Inspiration for a Ridiculously Good Life," "Unstoppable: The Incredible Power of Faith in Action," "Love Without Limits," and many more. Additionally, he starred in a short film titled "The Butterfly Circus."

From Nick Vujicic's example, we can understand that success or failure does not depend on the body's shortcomings or others' love or trust in us. By comprehending the importance of life and by changing our perspective, we can quickly overcome depression and make a fresh start.

 Set this book aside for a few moments and reflect on your positive qualities.

One beautiful way to nurture self-love is to develop self-respect. Here, respect means "re-spect", i.e., reassessing our own worth. It involves asking ourselves questions and taking steps toward self-improvement. We must seek out positive aspects about ourselves in every area of our lives, whether social, physical, mental, financial, or spiritual, and love ourselves by appreciating those positive attributes.

It is essential that people who love themselves also take care of their bodies lovingly.

Do you love your body?   ☐ Yes / ☐ No

Have you ever said, "I love you" to your body?   ☐ Yes / ☐ No

Have you ever expressed gratitude toward your body for being at your service 24 hours a day without stopping?   ☐ Yes / ☐ No

Regardless of your answer, let's perform an experiment now. Gently place your hand over your heart and tell your body, "I love you. I love you as you are. Thank you very much for always being with me."

Repeat this sentence five times while caressing your head with your hand.

 How do you feel after this exercise?

Indeed, your body understands everything about you and can feel your love. Hence, it is crucial to fulfill all your responsibilities toward your body by making changes in your exercise routine, health habits, and diet from time to time. It is through this body that you are living life, and a healthy body plays a vital role in living a long, healthy life.

Furthermore, on a mental and spiritual level, those who aspire to live a successful life always choose to stay happy. They choose to ignore minor incidents for the sake of their mental peace rather than constantly pondering over them.

 Therefore, take a moment to reflect on when you function happily and peacefully and when you don't.

To bless yourself with love, joy, and peace, meditate for some time every day, or nurture a hobby and become thoroughly engrossed in it. This is the time when you live for yourself and are with yourself.

At the financial and social level, reflect on what you currently have. It could be your house, car, mobile phone, or other small or big items. Make a list of all of them. Now, consider your relationships with friends and family who make you feel good. Create a list of those individuals as well. Feel grateful toward all of them and express your gratitude.

 You may set the book aside and thank each one, saying, "Thank you for being in my life."

 How do you feel after this exercise?

Bear in mind that you are performing all these exercises and actions for your own happiness.

There are many ways to shower yourself with love. It is not always necessary to verbalize it in words. Love is demonstrated through your actions when you embrace your imperfections, tend to your physical and mental well-being, express gratitude for every blessing and achievement, feel a surge of pride for your good deeds, and wholeheartedly accept yourself just as you are. In these moments, you genuinely feel an outpouring of love for yourself.

Love is akin to honey, inundated with a natural sweetness that needs no additional additives. Just as a flower does not rely on others to release its fragrance but spreads its aroma with a gentle breeze, similarly, one who loves oneself does not subject oneself to anguish. Regardless of whether they receive love from others, they do not depend on others. Instead, they radiate love like the fragrance in the air.

7

Even This Will Pass Away

In the previous session, we discussed the importance of loving ourselves So, have you begun to love yourself? ☐ Yes / ☐ No / ☐ A little.

Even if you are able to love yourself a bit at the moment, it is not a problem. Gradually, it can grow.

Let's begin today's session with a game of "Who Wants to Be a Millionaire." You will be asked a series of questions, and your task is to respond quickly without overthinking. Are you ready?

- As a child, did you experience anxiety or stress before exams? ☐ Yes / ☐ No
- Did that anxiety fade after the exams were over, bringing a sense of relief? ☐ Yes / ☐ No
- Did your heart race anxiously, waiting for the results to be announced? ☐ Yes / ☐ No
- Did you find solace after the results were announced? ☐ Yes / ☐ No
- Did you feel stress when trying to establish your career path, whether it's finding a job or starting a business? ☐ Yes / ☐ No
- And did that stress gradually dissipate as everything fell into place, leaving you with a newfound sense of calm? ☐ Yes / ☐ No

- Did you feel anxious before organizing an event at home or delivering a presentation at work? ☐ Yes / ☐ No

- Did the anxiety dissipate once the event or presentation was over? ☐ Yes / ☐ No

- Have all the tensions, sorrows, and disappointments you have experienced so far passed away? ☐ Yes / ☐ No

- So, do you feel confident that whatever sorrow or disappointment you are currently experiencing will also pass away? ☐ Yes / ☐ No

Great job! You have done well. It is good to see your confidence. The purpose of asking all these questions was to help you understand that situations are temporary. Storms come and go not only in your life but in everyone's. Many calamities have occurred and passed in society, the country, and the world as a whole.

Reflect on all the events in your life, whether they were pleasant or challenging. They have all passed! It is the law of nature that nothing lasts forever. Change is a beautiful law of nature. Change is permanent; it never stops. Just as morning follows night, spring follows winter, sorrow follows joy, and sorrow eventually gives way to joy again.

There must be numerous problems from the past that no longer exist today. Many things that exist today that didn't exist earlier. Our lives are constantly changing, but we often become aware of the change only when it becomes significant.

Is the current state of your mind the same as it has been since the beginning?

No! With each passing year, certain changes occur that cannot be stopped. Similarly, problems or troubling situations, as well as our emotions, are in a state of constant flux. However, if our mind is ready to embrace these changes with proper understanding, it becomes much easier to say, **"Even this will pass away."**

Let's adopt "Even this will pass away" as a little mantra. To reinforce the belief that the future holds the best for us, let's add, "Only the best times await us." Then, every moment of life will be filled with happiness. Whenever you feel sad, disheartened, demotivated, or despondent, remember this mantra: **"Even this will pass away, and only the best times await us."**

For instance, everyone must have experienced this during the Covid-19 pandemic. Those who had the understanding and faith that the pandemic would soon come to an end could cope calmly. Conversely, those who harbored doubts, such as, "I don't know how long this will last; How many years we will have to endure it," fell prey to fear or depression.

After any adversity strikes, everything becomes chaotic, but nothing will change if people merely lament while watching the scene. The storm will pass! Now, everyone should work together to fix things. Similarly, problems come and go in life. If you understand how to manage them, you can overcome any kind of depression because time does not stop; it passes. You should also accept that all the troubles caused by problems are bound to end one day.

 Now, recall and describe a problem you faced in the past that made you feel disappointed, sad, and discouraged at that time but has now come to an end.

The events in your life occur to give momentum to your stalled life. So, will you embrace them positively or let them weigh you down? If you want to take advantage of them, use this mantra: "Even this will pass away, and only the best times await us."

Dwelling on bad memories of the past only brings sorrow. Sorrow is nothing but a thought that intensifies when emotions are attached to it, bringing the bad memories to life. If we cling to those thoughts, they create a heap of sorrow. Many people have cultivated a habit of worrying and are constantly engrossed in worrying about one thing or another.

Losing a loved one can be a challenging experience, and the grieving process requires considerable time and effort. For instance, a doctor lost his wife. Despite his best efforts, he could not move past his grief, feeling as though he was trapped in a never-ending cycle of pain and sadness.

Determined to find a way out of this rut, he sought advice from his psychiatrist friend. After listening to the doctor's story and understanding the gravity of his pain, the psychiatrist offered a different perspective. "It is understandable to feel lost and overwhelmed right now after going through such an incident," he said. "However, time does not stop. Just as good times have passed, even this difficult time will pass. You cannot fill the void created by your wife's demise, but it is not wise to mourn your entire life. Remember that grief is a process that takes time to work through. Accept it. Instead of forcing yourself to move on immediately, allow your emotions to flow; develop a sense of comfort with your emotions, knowing that even they will pass."

The doctor found solace in his friend's advice. With time, patience, and a willingness to work through his grief, he eventually found a sense of peace and acceptance. While he never forgot his wife, he could move ahead and find joy in life once again.

It is natural to want to hold onto our grief when we experience loss or trauma, but time is a powerful healer. While some injuries may heal faster than others, ultimately, all wounds have the potential to heal. The same is true with our emotional wounds. With time and the right approach, we can learn to find peace and acceptance, even in the face of significant loss.

 Take a moment to reflect on the problems, worries, and troubles you are currently facing and write them down.

Always remember that no problem can be bigger than your morale. If your morale is high, every problem can be solved. Just get your mind to understand that "Whatever is happening now is going to pass, and only the best times await us."

Incorporate this mantra into your daily routine and notice its positive impact on your life. Thank you!

8

Outlook and Overlook With Patience

Hello! How is it going?

 Please share three positive things that have happened this week.

Good! Today, we will delve into another perspective that can significantly change how we perceive ourselves, others, our problems, and the world around us. However, it is essential to remember that a degree of patience is required in tandem with this approach.

Patience is not something that can be bought; it needs to be cultivated within ourselves. Before we move further, let's engage in a brief round of questions and answers:

- Have you ever observed ants carrying food particles like sugar, lentils, or rice grains in an organized line? ☐ Yes / ☐ No
- Are you familiar with the tale of the race between the tortoise and the hare? ☐ Yes / ☐ No
- Have you ever seen a dam? ☐ Yes / ☐ No

You might be wondering why these seemingly childlike unrelated questions are being asked and how they relate to depression.

The answers to these questions impart valuable lessons about patience. Each of us undergoes a wide range of life experiences, encompassing both joy and sorrow, ups and downs. When faced with sadness or disappointment, we occasionally become impatient and hastily make decisions that can adversely affect our personal relationships and professional work. Hence, it is vital to nurture patience during these challenging times.

For instance, ants patiently collect food to prepare for the rainy season. The timeless fable of the tortoise and the hare also teaches us that "Slow and steady wins the race."

We can learn invaluable lessons from nature itself. During the rainy season, people employ various techniques to manage rainwater. In some places, they construct earthen mounds to halt the water flow; in others, they use sandbags to impede rainwater during hurricanes. Dams are another example; they are built to amass and control water in one location, utilizing their energy to generate electricity. These examples demonstrate the significant value of patiently accumulating energy resources in one place and channeling them for development.

In nature, we observe plants, trees, and birds exhibit patience in their own unique way. A plant doesn't rush to bear fruit or bloom; it patiently waits for the right time. Trees exhibit unwavering patience, waiting for years to blossom and bear fruit. Birds painstakingly and meticulously build their nests, adding one twig at a time, patiently creating a home for their offspring. It is primarily humans who seem to lack the virtue of patience. We often desire instant gratification, whether it is a home, wealth, or material comforts. We tend to approach tasks with an expectation of immediate results, akin to the services of Aladdin's genie, and then feel disheartened when our expectations are not met.

Nonetheless, by gleaning wisdom from the natural world around us and embracing patience in our own lives, we can foster a more meaningful and fulfilling existence.

 Reflect on your daily life and identify areas where incorporating more patience could lead to greater satisfaction and success.

We often become so engulfed in our problems and dilemmas that we lose patience. Yet, it is paramount to cultivate the virtue of patience, as a lack of it can prove catastrophic in certain situations.

It is commonly observed that even minor setbacks can trigger a storm of negative thoughts, leading to chaos. If left unchecked, this deluge of thoughts can lead to depression or even thoughts of self-harm and suicide.

For instance, when a river dam collapses, the ensuing flood can wreak havoc on surrounding villages, fields, and cities, necessitating a significant amount of time to restore normalcy.

Similarly, when negative thoughts remain unchecked, they can trigger a cascade of thoughts that can disrupt one's mental and physical well-being, impairing the power of discernment and intellect. Just as a dam is necessary on a river to efficiently harness every drop of water, it is vital to construct a dam of patience over the stream of thoughts so that one can calmly navigate through every problem.

 Developing patience in everyday, minor situations can act as a shield against a range of mental illnesses like stress and depression. As the saying goes, "The fruits of patience are sweet." What has been your experience in this regard?

It can be challenging to be patient and persevere in some situations. However, if we practice them in trivial everyday situations, we will also reap their benefits in significant incidents.

For instance, imagine you are trying to learn a new skill, such as playing a musical instrument. In the beginning, it can be both frustrating and challenging. You might require assistance to hit the right notes or play in rhythm with the music. However, with diligent and patient practice, you will gradually improve. Eventually, you will be able to perform more complex compositions and express yourself more fully through your music. In contrast, without patience, you might abandon the instrument altogether, missing out on the joy and satisfaction that comes with mastering a new skill.

Let's consider another example. You have an important presentation at work scheduled in just an hour. You decide to grab some coffee from the kitchen, but unfortunately, the coffee machine is out of order. You then attempt to print your presentation, only to discover that the printer doesn't work. Despite your efforts to reach technical support, you can't seem to get through. These situations can lead to frustration and impatience, potentially causing your "dam of patience" to rupture.

Similarly, when you send an urgent text message, and the other person does not respond promptly, it can make your mind restless. You might also find yourself growing impatient and anxious when public transport, like trains or buses, runs late. However, if you make a habit of practicing patience every day, you enhance your ability to remain calm even during stressful events.

Now, the question arises, "How can I cultivate patience?"

Do you have any techniques to cultivate patience? ☐ Yes / ☐ No

If your answer is "Yes," please write down what you can do to practice and cultivate patience.

Good! Now, let's try to incorporate the concept of the tortoise, which symbolizes patience. The two eyes of the tortoise point to changing our outlook and overlooking situations.

Change your outlook!

As you might have observed, the tortoise advances by keeping its ultimate goal in mind, consistently focusing on steady growth. While its development may occur at a slow pace, it never comes to a halt.

Likewise, regardless of the situations we encounter, it is essential to maintain our focus on our ultimate goal and growth or to consider altering our perspective when dealing with these situations.

For instance, if someone at home or in the office criticizes your work or highlights your flaws, practicing patience can help you remain composed and open to feedback. Instead of reacting defensively or becoming frustrated, take a deep breath and try to listen to their input without passing judgment. Pose questions to yourself like, "What can I learn from this? Which qualities can I nurture within myself to promote personal growth?"

This change in outlook can help you cultivate patience in such situations and transform criticism into an opportunity for self-improvement and personal growth. This can be achieved only when you maintain your focus on your ultimate goal and growth.

Similarly, when you are stuck in heavy traffic on your way to an important appointment, it is natural to feel frustrated and impatient. However, practicing patience allows you to turn this time to your advantage. You can utilize this time to listen to a podcast, an audiobook, or relaxing music to soothe your mind, or you could plan your day's schedule, effectively turning an aggravating situation into a productive one.

This understanding can make you more perceptive when you encounter such situations, as it encourages a shift in your outlook. The kind of perspective we hold influences the thoughts that emerge within us, ultimately shaping our disposition as optimists or pessimists.

Ask yourself, "Do I have an optimistic or a pessimistic outlook?"

Overlook your perspective!

Sometimes, we may find it difficult to change our outlook in some situations despite our best efforts. At such times, we should adopt the second quality of the tortoise - overlooking. Like the tortoise, we should keep moving forward on our path, overlooking and disregarding the distractions around us.

For instance, when someone fails to acknowledge your efforts, speaks ill of you, or criticizes you, you should continue moving forward at your own pace, paying no heed to their negativity. In other words, you should overlook certain things, much like the tortoise.

Suppose you have been called for an important office meeting and you arrive ten minutes late. You realize the meeting has already started, and you feel bad you were late. But if you have the quality of overlooking, you will quickly settle down, organize your thoughts, and contribute effectively to the meeting.

 Reflect on aspects of your daily life that you should overlook but find it difficult to do so.

It is commendable that you are engaging in self-reflection and recognizing the need to practice patience, change your outlook, and overlook certain things.

When you learn the art of overlooking, you become better equipped to understand others' perspectives. By nurturing this small but valuable skill, you can enrich your relationships. More importantly, you remain calm and content within, far from your despair, where there is no room for depression. You are responsible for your happiness; no one can take it away from you.

In the next session, we will learn a practical way of exercising patience. Until then, try to identify opportunities in your daily life, as trivial as they may be, where you can practice patience, change your outlook, and overlook certain things. Thank you!

9

It's Just a Matter Of ----

As learned in the previous session, were you able to observe patience in various situations? ☐ Yes / ☐ No

Were you able to practice overlooking in some situations and changing your outlook in some other situations? ☐ Yes / ☐ No

It is truly inspiring to see your passion for continuous learning and your ability to grasp and apply new concepts quickly. In this session, we will learn a mantra that can help enhance your patience, hoping that it will enable you to maintain composure in challenging situations.

As we cultivate more patience within ourselves, we become better equipped to tackle any task or challenge, reducing the likelihood of rushing through our activities. Before we dive into the session, let's take a moment to assess your current level of patience.

 How would you rate your patience on a scale of 1 to 10, with 1 being the lowest and 10 being the highest?

Regardless of the current rating, let's work on enhancing our patience level.

Negative thoughts, when deeply ingrained, often play a significant role in causing depression. Changing these thought patterns requires the essential quality of patience, allowing one to find peace and calm within oneself.

By practicing patience, we become more adept at accepting any situation that comes our way, which can help us overcome feelings of depression or negativity.

Let's understand this with an example. Imagine your children express a strong desire to go to a circus or a fair located quite far away. While you may not have a personal interest in the circus or the fair, with patience, you decide to take your children and truly enjoy the day with them. You fulfill their every wish, be it trying to shoot at balloons, riding camels, making stops at various stalls and vendors, or admiring toys. With great patience, you take them around, and as the day unfolds, your tired children eventually fall asleep on your lap. Even then, you patiently carry them home. During this time, there is no tension or negative thoughts in your mind; your sole purpose is to happily fulfill your children's desires and enjoy the time together.

For instance, consider a situation where your child is struggling to learn a specific skill, like riding a bike. Without patience, you might become frustrated with their progress and perhaps start criticizing them or discontinuing your support. Such actions can negatively impact your child's self-esteem and confidence, potentially discouraging them from continuing to practice and learn. However, when you approach the situation with patience and clarity, you can provide essential support and encouragement to your child. You can take the time to explain things in a way that suits their understanding and offer positive feedback for their efforts. This approach can boost their confidence and motivation to persist in their learning.

Practicing patience is not only vital for our well-being but also for the well-being of those we care about, especially our children. Parents, in particular, face numerous challenges and difficulties in raising their children, and patience is a key factor in effectively handling these challenges. By cultivating patience, parents can not only find their way out of depression but also assist their children in building self-confidence and a positive outlook on life.

Recall a moment when things didn't go as planned, but you managed to stay completely calm without feeling tense, anxious, or afraid. Please take a moment to write it down.

We must practice patience, even in the face of minor annoyances. For instance, when working on a computer and experiencing frequent crashes or overheating, or when the air conditioner fails to work, or when dining at a restaurant and the food arrives late, it can easily provoke irritation.

Part of learning patience is learning to ignore or overlook. For example, when encountering comments or dislikes on social media, it is essential to remember the phrase, "Do not dislike the dislikes and do not like the likes." This means accepting these reactions as they are and choosing to overlook them.

We don't have comprehensive knowledge of everything happening worldwide, yet life continues. Similarly, what your neighbor thinks of you, even if you remain unaware of it for the rest of your life, ultimately doesn't matter. People may harbor negative thoughts about you, and it can be distressing when you discover that someone is speaking ill of you behind your back. In such situations, it is better not to attach significance to these occurrences but instead to overlook them. With practice and patience, this becomes easier over time.

Even a simple mantra phrase can be remarkably effective. Consider the phrase: **"It's just a matter of ----."** You can fill in the blank with words that suit the situation and invoke patience within you. For instance, "It's just a matter of a few moments...," "It's just a matter of a few days...," "It's just a matter of making some effort...," "It's just a matter of summoning courage," and so on.

For instance, if you are sitting in the dark due to an electric power outage and feeling fearful and irritable, instead of blaming the situation, you can tell yourself, "It's just a matter of a few moments."

When you are apprehensive about the pain of a doctor's injection, you can remind yourself, "It's just a matter of a few moments of pain." As mentioned earlier, you can customize this phrase with words that resonate with your situation.

If someone in your household is unwell, and you need to care for them, you can say, "It's just a matter of some time or a few months." This can replace the stress with an attitude of acceptance, enabling you to give care with patience.

So, whenever you find yourself on the verge of losing patience, remind yourself of this mantra phrase. Tailor the phrase to suit your specific circumstances, and you will be amazed at how much easier it becomes to practice patience.

Reflect on the situations where you can make use of this mantra. Write down the situations and the specific mantra phrase you would use in each situation.

Cultivating patience is a skill that requires practice, and regularly using mantra phrases like "It's just a matter of…" can help us gradually develop a more patient attitude.

It is crucial to understand that patience doesn't mean passively accepting whatever comes our way without seeking to improve it. Sometimes, taking action and actively working to enhance our circumstances is necessary. However, by nurturing patience, we can approach these challenges with a clearer, more composed mindset, which increases our effectiveness in addressing them.

Biographies of successful people provide valuable insights into their struggles and how they persevered through adversities with patience. Despite encountering setbacks and failures, these individuals remained committed to their goals and eventually reaped the rewards of their determination. Even in the face of depression, many successful individuals maintained their focus and successfully overcame their adversities.

The reality is that there are no shortcuts to success. Patience is an essential ingredient in achieving one's goals, and it demands ongoing effort and unwavering dedication over time. To adopt this mindset, we can incorporate a mantra phrase into our daily lives and commit to reading the biographies of remarkable individuals. This practice can fortify our determination and help us develop the patience needed to achieve our goals.

Continue using the mantra phrase until our next session and delve into the biography of one of your favorite great personalities. This exploration will provide insight into how they navigated life's challenges and steadily ascended to greater heights, one step at a time, through their patience and determination.

10

Focusing on Purposeful Actions

 In our previous session, we discussed a mantra you could apply in various situations. Did you get a chance to try it out? If yes, how did it go?

It is good to hear that you have been integrating this mantra into your life. Keep practicing it, as it can prove valuable at various junctures in life! Small steps pave the way for significant achievements. They can help you in shifting your focus away from depression.

Those struggling with depression often feel confused, with their thoughts in a constant state of flux, running helter-skelter. Consequently, they find it challenging to focus on their work or deal with life's challenges without being overwhelmed by negative thoughts.

 It is essential to observe yourself and your thoughts. When negative thoughts arise, do you tend to get caught up in them, or do you strive to redirect your focus elsewhere?

It has been observed that those with depression often get entangled in negative thoughts, sinking deeper into them instead of trying to redirect their focus. However, learning to defocus is crucial for them to make room to concentrate on the positive aspects.

If you want to focus on positivity, you must learn to defocus first. Imagine a container filled with milk. It can only hold a limited amount before overflowing. Until it is emptied, more milk cannot be added. Similarly, to make room for fresh, new thoughts, you must clear out the accumulated clutter of negative thoughts in your mind and try something different.

If you dwell on why you feel depressed and how it developed, you will find yourself trapped in a whirlpool of thoughts, unable to find an escape. However, shifting your focus on learning something new or nurturing a hobby can significantly increase your chances of overcoming depression.

 What kind of work or hobby would you like to nurture and focus on?

Let's also understand the rationale behind this. According to the Laws of Thought, "What we focus on manifests in our life and multiplies." If we focus on fear, distress, negativity, or failure, these situations will manifest in our life. Conversely, if we focus on health, growth, positivity, or success, they will manifest in our life.

One may question how a person grappling with depression can defocus. However, it is crucial to understand that we can achieve defocusing not just mentally but also physically by engaging in some physical activities.

Learn something new or rekindle a hobby

Many of us had hobbies like painting, photography, cooking, cycling, music, or dancing during childhood. Some people enjoy hiking, reading books, learning languages, sightseeing, exploring health therapies, or going to the gym. If you didn't have time or opportunity to pursue these hobbies earlier, you can pursue them now. You can also enroll in an online or offline course to learn something new.

Engaging in such hobbies can alleviate your sorrow, keep you rooted in the present, and contribute to your growth. They can also rekindle rich memories from your childhood and help you become free from negative thoughts.

 Recall any of your childhood hobbies and jot down the steps to reengage in them.

Now, put these hobbies into practice. You may also consider childhood games like Hoola Hoop, rope skipping, or solving brainteasers as part of your hobbies.

Exploring various forms of therapy

Our old behavioral patterns can make us more susceptible to feelings of sadness. Instead, we should explore new avenues and adopt positive thinking to reduce stress and anxiety, making us feel more contented.

As we shift our focus, it automatically initiates the healing process. Learning healing therapies like BFT (Bach Flower Therapy), EFT (Emotional Freedom Technique), water therapy, color therapy, Reiki, Pranic healing, Yoga, and Pranayama can be incredibly beneficial. We can practice these techniques for our own benefit as well as for helping others. Sharing the benefits of these therapies and the thought of helping others can inspire us to overcome depression. However, it is essential to make ourselves healthy first before helping others effectively.

Engaging in impersonal service

Engaging in impersonal service can also help us shift our focus away from depression and foster our personal growth. You may join a group that focuses on positive aspects or volunteer for a non-profit organization dedicated to child education, social service, or spiritual growth. Through this engagement, when you see the sufferings and hardships of others, you will experience compassion for them, which you were otherwise seeking for yourself from others. You may realize, "My problems are insignificant compared to the challenges and hardships others face. I unnecessarily dwell on minor issues and suffer." This shift in perspective can change how you perceive sorrow, leading you toward growth.

Have you ever participated in impersonal service, such as volunteering for an NGO or community service organization? If so, how did it make you feel, and did it help shift your focus from your problems to the needs of others?

Taking out time for exercise

Look around and observe how happy people live their lives. Many start their day with activities such as exercises, brisk walking, jogging, yoga, meditation, or by joining a laughing club. This routine helps them feel refreshed and energized throughout the day, setting a positive tone for their day. It allows them to remain cheerful and maintain high energy levels. Consider incorporating these activities into your morning routine to improve your physical and mental well-being.

Until our next session, reflect on the discussions from this session and start making positive changes in your life.

11

Harnessing Nature's Healing Power

Do you acknowledge the divine providence that functions through nature? ☐ Yes / ☐ No

Are you familiar with the benefits of Naturopathy? ☐ Yes / ☐ No

In ancient times, people were more conscious about their health. They understood well that if their body were healthy, they would be mentally healthy, and vice versa. They had a profound understanding of the connection between a healthy body and a healthy mind. Working outdoors, breathing fresh air, doing physical exercises, basking in sunlight, and nurturing the environment, including the flora and fauna, were part of their daily lifestyle. The use of machines was minimal.

Whenever they fell ill, they would treat themselves with medicinal herbs and natural home remedies. Moreover, they were more socially connected. Due to their strong familial bonds, they would openly discuss every matter and every problem within their families. As a result, they didn't experience much stress or depression in those times.

However, with time, significant changes have occurred. In the modern era of urbanization and technological advancement, people have moved away from nature. Nuclear families, processed foods, polluted air and water, stressful workplaces, unhealthy diets, and indiscriminate indulgence in gadgets and social media have become a part of life. This has led to various physical ailments and emotional upheavals like anxiety, prolonged stress, and disharmony in relationships, leading to depression.

But nature has so many inherent qualities that even if one goes for the holistic approach of naturopathy, it not only addresses depression but also helps overcome a wide range of physical ailments. When there is an imbalance in the natural ecosystem, nature restores balance in its own natural way. Similarly, the human body, too, has been bestowed with the innate intelligence to heal itself. When there is a disease, the body can treat itself.

Have you ever considered incorporating natural remedies and practices into your health routine? ☐ Yes / ☐ No

Are you open to exploring alternative therapies, like naturopathy, for promoting overall well-being? ☐ Yes / ☐ No

Everything in nature is abundant with healthy qualities, be it fruits, vegetables, water, pure air, sunlight, or plants. These invaluable resources are vital for our physical and mental well-being. The best part is that most of them are freely bestowed upon us as gifts from nature. Even our basic body functions like breathing, resting, sleeping, and even smiling are gifts we often overlook. We need to take the help of the essential gifts of nature, such as, sunlight, air, and water, to combat depression.

Sunlight

Sunlight is a natural source of energy that evokes joy and enthusiasm within us. When we don't get enough sunlight, we often feel dull and sad, akin to how we feel during the rainy season when the sky is clouded, and sunlight doesn't reach the Earth for a long time. This condition is also referred to as Seasonal Affective Disorder (SAD). Therefore, it is essential to ensure that we get adequate exposure to sunlight to keep our minds and bodies healthy.

Depression often manifests as a state of darkness, but exposure to sunlight can help alleviate its grip. Even 10 minutes of sunlight twice daily can have a rejuvenating effect on us.

Moreover, sunlight activates the neurotransmitter serotonin in the brain, which helps maintain a positive mood. Sunlight can be especially beneficial for individuals whose emotional state is affected by their atmosphere, like the lack of exposure to sunlight.

The Sun gives life to the entire Earth. It directly impacts our bodies as the energy emitted by the Sun enhances our mental and physical resilience. One practice that harnesses the power of the Sun is *Tratak* meditation, in which we concentrate our gaze steadily upon the rising or setting Sun without blinking our eyes.

Have you ever explored Tratak meditation or any other practices that involve harnessing the power of the Sun? ☐ Yes / ☐ No

If you haven't tried it before, consider starting with 30 seconds and gradually increasing to 15 minutes. This is subject to your comfort level in gazing at the Sun as in some parts of the world, it may not be possible to gaze at the Sun for a prolonged period.

Water

Water holds significant importance for our mental and physical well-being. Even for those who don't particularly enjoy it, deliberately maintaining contact with water is crucial, as avoiding it may invite feelings of sadness. Water assumes the color that is added to it. Hence, think positively when you drink water to add positivity to it; water absorbs the energy of our thoughts. Take a moment to sit, relax, and slowly drink water whenever you are thirsty while affirming positive statements to yourself, such as "I am pure, serene, and balanced."

An effective practice to balance the chakras (energy vortices) in your body involves keeping a glass filled with water in sunlight for a couple of days and then drinking that water.

Water is an integral part of our lives, and some people find solace in spending a significant time, being in contact with water.

Considering the season, how often do you come in contact with water in a day? How much water do you drink daily?

Just as about 70% of the Earth's surface is water, similarly, about 70% of our body is also made of water. It is an inseparable part of life itself. It is advised to drink 2 to 3 liters of water daily to cleanse the body. Further, this is also subject to your comfort level in drinking water. People in colder regions or seasons may not be comfortable drinking so much water.

Whenever we take a bath, it not only refreshes our body but also rejuvenates our mind. Therefore, it is essential to bathe twice daily for mental peace, adjusting the frequency according to the weather.

Exercise and *Pranayama*

Just as sunlight and water are essential for our body, so is oxygen. Oxygen plays a crucial role in our well-being. Hence, it is beneficial to engage in activities such as walking in the fresh air, exercising, practicing Pranayama, and spending time in open spaces, gardens, or natural surroundings to experience mental peace.

You may incorporate Pranayama exercises like *Anulom-Vilom* Pranayama (alternate nostril breathing), *Bhramari* Pranayama, and *Ujjayi* Pranayama into your daily routine to help reduce depression. Practicing them for 20 minutes twice daily can be effective.

Practicing Pranayama opens all the pores of the body, facilitating the release of toxins in the form of sweat. As you focus on breathing, you become aware of the present moment and live a mindful life in the present. Those who experience depression should pay attention to their breathing during moments of grief. With this, they can quickly alleviate sad feelings.

 Now, take deep breaths and inhale and exhale five times. Observe your breathing for 1 or 2 minutes.

Diet

It is essential to have a well-balanced diet as part of our daily meals because deficiencies of vitamins A, C, E, or iron can aggravate depression. If you include green vegetables, salads, lentils, and fruits in your diet, they play an important role in balancing your body and mind.

Foods rich in magnesium, such as leafy vegetables, beans, nuts, seeds, and whole grains, as well as zinc-rich foods like egg yolks, cashews, etc., help us remain calm.

Low-fat dairy products, broccoli, cabbage, cauliflower, bitter gourd, sprouts, cucumber, apples, dark chocolate, bananas, kiwi, *Jamun*, *Shatavari*, and antioxidant-rich foods like avocado and cherry tomatoes are very useful. Green tea and Kombucha tea help in boosting immunity.

It is advisable to refrain from consuming certain items such as sugar, simple carbohydrates, bakery products, caffeine, alcohol, and non-vegetarian food.

 Considering the type of food included in your diet, do you prefer junk food or home-cooked meals?

When you feel sad, do you feel the urge to eat something?

☐ Yes / ☐ No

When experiencing deep sadness, it is advisable to neither overeat nor skip meals. If your appetite is low, opt for mild and easily digestible foods like soups, porridge, lentil soup, and rice until your appetite returns to normal.

Despite the inclination to avoid nature during bouts of depression, spending time in natural surroundings can enhance both your physical and mental well-being. Deliberately basking in sunlight, engaging with water, exercising, and maintaining a balanced diet can boost your overall productivity. Make a conscious effort to modify your daily routines, stay connected with nature, and share your experiences with others. This will help you overcome depression, and gradually, depression will begin to lose its grip.

12

Reclaim Your Inherent Joy and Passion

Today's weather is delightful. Why not make the most of this beautiful day by taking a stroll in the fields of the countryside?

Feeling a bit puzzled? Don't worry! We are not physically going anywhere. We are simply using our imagination to transport ourselves to the fields.

Visualize yourself in a charming village surrounded by lush green fields with crops gently swaying in the breeze. Along the roadside, trees are laden with fruits, their branches gracefully bending down as if to welcome you. Birds fill the air with cheerful chirping. The pleasant, gentle breeze caresses you and whispers in your ears. While walking, you pause near a mango tree, pluck a mango, and take a bite. Unfortunately, the mango tastes bitter, and you quickly spit it out.

You can't help but wonder if there is something wrong with your taste buds. Disappointed, you discard the first mango and select another. However, to your dismay, the second mango is even more bitter.

While you stand puzzled by this unexpected bitter flavor, you notice a farmer approaching you. Out of curiosity, you ask him why the mangoes taste bitter.

The farmer explains that the roots of a neem tree (a tree native to the Indian continent) had been intertwined with those of the mango tree. The farmer who had planted the mango tree didn't tend to its surroundings, allowing a neem tree to share common ground with the mango tree.

Thus, the bitterness of the neem tree affected the mango tree. How can the fruit be sweet when the roots are bitter?

 This story serves as a simple example, highlighting an important lesson. Regardless of its realism, what metaphorical message can you draw from it?

Certainly! If we want a sweet fruit, even its roots should be in favorable surroundings. Now, let's explore how this analogy relates to our minds.

When one grows up in a hostile environment, negativity infests their thoughts. When these thoughts are left unattended without any effort to change them, their roots become strong and penetrate deep into their minds. They manifest sometimes in situations or show up during their interactions with others, taint their personality, and consequently fill their life with bitterness. Quietly, these roots of negativity spread within them. If they disregard these signs and make no effort to change their thoughts, they may find themselves spiraling into depression over time.

 Recall a childhood incident that triggered negative emotions within you and lingered for a long time. Remember someone's negative behavior toward you that deeply saddened you. Later, you always harbored negative thoughts toward that person. Do you still feel anger when you see them?

Let's explore this further using an example. Consider a family with three children—two girls and a boy—living with their parents in a low-income setting. Despite being the youngest, the boy was burdened with the expectation of assuming responsibility for the family solely because of his gender. Like other children, he was mischievous and more focused on playing sports and having fun. However, his father would often beat him because of his behavior, while his family members would frequently criticize him, labeling him as worthless, foolish, and irresponsible. Consequently, the boy's mind was filled with resentment towards his parents and sisters. Although he outwardly appeared calm, internally, he harbored negative thoughts about everyone.

As he grew up, he became engrossed in his work. Yet unknowingly, he would end up engaging in conflicts with others, misinterpreting their intentions as wrong and selfish. Unfortunately, no one tried to understand him or make him understand. With time, the feelings of hatred transformed into anger and disgust. Eventually, the young boy became entangled in vices and sank into depression.

The above example vividly illustrates that if the boy had been guided properly during his formative years, he would not have fallen prey to depression.

 Please take a moment to reflect on your thoughts and observe how your thoughts are predominantly guided. What is the proportion of positive thoughts vis-a-vis negative thoughts within you?

If your thoughts tend to be negative, there is often a reason behind it. In today's world, our thinking has become increasingly influenced by the internet and the media. News channels continuously broadcast negative news throughout the day, while entertainment channels predominantly promote negative thinking. This constant exposure to negativity shrouds our joy, progressive thoughts, and contentment. Given this, it is essential to proactively cultivate positive thoughts instead of remaining trapped in negative thoughts. Let's understand this with the help of another example.

Imagine a young artist named Rachana, who is deeply passionate about painting. As a child, her creativity knew no bounds. She would spend hours happily exploring colors, experimenting with various techniques, and relishing the joy of self-expression through art.

Rachana's early years were marked by a mixture of positive and negative thoughts. There were moments when she doubted her abilities and felt frustrated when her artistic vision didn't quite match the outcome. However, these negative thoughts were fleeting, as Rachana would quickly immerse herself in the sheer delight of creating.

As Rachana grew older, external influences began to play a more significant role in shaping her perception of art. She encountered critical feedback, comparisons to other artists, and the pressure to conform to certain styles or expectations. Over time, these experiences began to overshadow the positive aspects of her creative journey. Negative thoughts about her skills and self-worth took hold, while the joy and freedom she once felt started to fade into the background. Rachana became increasingly preoccupied with her perceived flaws and limitations, often dismissing her unique artistic voice.

Over time, Rachana became accustomed to this pattern of self-doubt and negativity. She started believing that her art could never meet the standards set by others, which led her to abandon projects or shy away from sharing her work with the world.

One day, while going through her belongings, Rachana stumbled upon a collection of her childhood paintings. As she gazed at the vibrant, uninhibited strokes of her younger self, a wave of nostalgia washed over her. At that moment, she realized how the weight of negative thoughts had clouded the purity of her early artistic journey.

Inspired by this rediscovery, Rachana consciously decided to reconnect with her positive thoughts and embrace the joy of creating without judgment. She sought out supportive communities, surrounded herself with uplifting influences, and embarked on a journey of self-acceptance and self-expression. Gradually, Rachana's creative spark reignited. She learned to embrace both the challenges and triumphs of her artistic process, recognizing that negative thoughts were merely obstacles that could be overcome with perseverance and a positive mindset.

In this example, Rachana's journey represents the typical pattern of focusing attention on negative thoughts as we age. However, by consciously recognizing and nurturing positive thoughts, we can reclaim the joy, passion, and self-belief that were once inherent in our childhood experiences.

Rachana's story reminds us that the power to change our mindset lies within us. We become what we focus on. By shifting our focus to the positive, we regain our confidence and rediscover the magic of embracing the full spectrum of our thoughts and experiences.

Now, let's reflect on a few questions:

Are you aware of your thoughts? ☐ Yes / ☐ No / ☐ Sometimes

Do you recognize your responsibility in overcoming depression?
☐ Yes / ☐ No

Are you ready to transform the deep-rooted thoughts within your mind?
☐ Yes / ☐ No

Initially, we may not realize that negative thoughts are lurking in the depths of our minds while we entertain positive thoughts on the surface. With negativity at the core, we tend to find problems in many situations we encounter and get disappointed with those around us, which, in turn, intensifies our sorrow and despair.

Negative thoughts are akin to wild weeds that sprout effortlessly in any setting without requiring nurturing. Conversely, cultivating positive thoughts resembles a farmer's toil in nurturing a bountiful crop. We must diligently nurture and strengthen positive thoughts by paying them due attention. Only then can we lead a truly happy life.

See you in the next session.

13

It Doesn't Matter

You appear cheerful today. Looks like much of your confusion has been resolved from the previous session and things are becoming clearer to you.

With today's session, you will gain even more clarity; we will discuss yet another mantra: **"It Doesn't Matter."**

Have you ever used or heard someone say this phrase before?

☐ Yes / ☐ No

"It Doesn't Matter" are three small words, but understanding their significance can give a new direction to your life and help solve your problems.

In our daily life, we come across situations where we were supposed to get something that we were looking forward to, but didn't. We visit someone and they don't treat us cordially. We propose a solution in a meeting, but that goes unnoticed, or we find people have made decisions without informing us. Our favorite team loses a match against its archrival. At such times, we feel incomplete, frustrated, dejected, or unworthy. We think we can be happy only if we get the desired outcome.

 If you have experienced similar situations, please write them down.

Now, let's consider some worrisome thoughts that can pop up and unsettle us. "What will happen if I go broke? What if I don't get a job? What if no one appreciates or acknowledges my contribution? What will happen if I put on weight? What if I don't score well? What if I fall sick? What will happen to me if I am left alone? What will I do if my friends and relatives are upset with me? How will I survive the rising inflation? What if I don't find the perfect life partner?" This list can go on.

Do any of these situations resonate with your own experience?

☐ Yes / ☐ No

If you have any other situations, please list them.

You may say that such concerns are common among most people, and indeed, you are not the only one experiencing them. However, these seemingly grave worries drain a significant amount of our energy. With every such incident or worry, our mind protests, "This shouldn't happen." This builds resistance within us and gathers the momentum of negative thoughts, disrupting our peace. If we don't keep a timely check on them, they can escalate to the point of causing depression.

At such times, we can repeat the magic sentence, "It Doesn't Matter." It serves as a force technique to pull the mind out of the quicksand of negative thoughts. When we emerge from the spiral of negative thoughts, we are better placed to accept those situations where the mind resists a possibility. The problem begins to dissolve. We can experience at least some relief if not instant happiness. Otherwise, the more we resist, the more we feel unhappy, leading to heaviness and gloom.

For example, when someone is unable to find a job, pondering on it repeatedly can halt their thinking process, and they can feel despondent. However, the moment they say, "It Doesn't Matter," they stop resisting the situation. They remain in the present moment and become receptive to the intuitive guidance coming from within and the subtle cues from nature. Their chances of stumbling upon the solution significantly improve.

Try using this phrase in your daily life incidents and observe the outcomes.

 Close your eyes and recall an old incident that made you feel terrible. Repeat the phrase, "It Doesn't Matter," multiple times.

 Share your experience with this exercise.

"It Doesn't Matter" can also be applied when you don't get what you desire. You wanted your manager to appreciate you, but he didn't. You wanted three days off, but you were granted only one.

Often, when you are unable to find an immediate solution to your problem, it is better to keep it aside for some time. The solution could hit you at the most unexpected moments such as when you are relaxed, taking a shower, strolling in the park, or engaged in a mundane conversation. Even the slightest clue can lead you toward the solution.

Many great scientists and inventors have used this method, whether knowingly or unknowingly. When faced with a particularly challenging problem and unable to find a solution, they set aside the problem for some time. It was during those vacant moments when their mind was not occupied with the problem, the solution suddenly and intuitively emerged.

Likewise, we can also apply the "It Doesn't Matter" mantra in situations where we lack clarity and our view is clouded. Leave aside the problem for some time. In a few days, you will be able to get some insight into the solution to your problem. It may come to you through some person, thought, or piece of information. Consequently, you will find a new way of solving it.

"It Doesn't Matter"—these three miraculous words help us to become stress-free. However, the mind doesn't take long to become entangled again. Hence, it is necessary to repeat "It Doesn't Matter" several times throughout the day to be free from any entanglement of the mind.

Just as we regularly clean the dust accumulated on various objects in our house, we need to cleanse our mind regularly. Whenever the mind starts thinking negatively, it starts gathering the dust of sorrow. Repeating this simple mantra can help declutter the mind.

You will come across many occasions when you can use this mantra to free your mind from problems. When we reconvene for the next session, share the contentment and joy you experienced.

14

Not a Big Deal

Today, you appear rejuvenated. It seems that the mantra "It Doesn't Matter" has worked wonders.

Undesirable things may happen, or desirable things may not happen. In both cases, it doesn't matter. Embrace freedom and live your life to the fullest. Letting go of thoughts about the past and future unburdens your mind and lightens your spirit. Whatever little burden is left can also diminish after this session.

Today, we will understand how to effectively manage our day-to-day life situations appropriately and efficiently use yet another magical phrase, **"Not a Big Deal."**

It is a common trait to make a mountain out of a molehill. People with this trait tend to magnify things that are not really critical and give them undue importance. When things do not turn out as they would prefer, resistance builds up within them. Gradually, they begin to fret. Even when served a full, delicious meal, their focus zooms in on a tiny aspect that puts them off. As a result, they ignore the sumptuous meal; being grateful is farfetched for them.

When everything else goes well in their life, they focus on trivial matters that are not going well and brood over them. It is the law of nature that whatever we focus on grows in our life. Therefore, they end up seeing even more undesirable incidents happening in their lives.

For instance, consider someone who accidentally misplaces their keys while rushing to leave the house in the morning. Instead of treating it as a minor inconvenience, they start to panic and think, "I'm so forgetful. I can never keep track of anything," or "This is a sign that today is an unlucky day," or "I'll be late for work, and my boss will be furious." By magnifying the significance of losing their keys, they inadvertently contribute to feelings of distress and frustration. As a result, they may continue to encounter similar instances of forgetfulness or misplacement of belongings. During such moments, it becomes crucial to shift their focus toward positive aspects and prevent such minor incidents from disrupting their overall well-being.

There is a saying that the fear of calamity is much grimmer than the calamity itself. Incidents happen spontaneously and naturally in life, but the mind can blow things out of proportion and present them in a magnified way.

It is akin to looking at an ant through a magnifying glass and perceiving it as a dinosaur. The mind views each incident through a magnifying glass, exaggerating things with unwavering confidence, leading us to believe its distorted version. This can cause turmoil over trivial matters. We rarely delve deeper into its claims, causing these incidents to become a source of depression.

Interestingly, people often use idiomatic expressions without intending to be taken literally. For instance, phrases like "My head feels like it's about to explode from this headache" or "I have eaten so much that my stomach is about to burst" are simply figures of speech used to convey strong emotions. It's understood that a head cannot explode, and a stomach cannot burst from overeating. Due to this, such expressions do not typically cause stress or disappointment to anyone. However, when a real-life incident occurs involving ourselves or others, our mind exaggerates similarly, leading us to easily fall into the trap of believing in its distorted interpretation.

Consider a family going on a trip filled with happiness and excitement, expecting a delightful holiday together. During the flight, they had big plans. However, after four hours in air, the flight was unable to land due to bad weather, forcing a return. Upon their return, the parents began complaining, "We planned our trip so meticulously and now it's been jeopardized," etc.

When you experience disappointment due to such incidents, you should say the magical phrase: "Not a Big Deal." As soon as you say it, your mind will receive a signal to stop grumbling. Then, immediately ask yourself, "What's the worst that can happen or could have happened?"

You will get the answer from within, just as the parents in the above incident did. "The weather could have worsened, and we could have been in danger. It's fortunate that we could return safely. If something had happened during the landing, it would have been unsafe," etc. Thus, "Not a Big Deal" helped them handle the situation.

Reflect upon the incidents that you exaggerate and upset you. Ask yourself, "Am I assigning an exaggerated value to these incidents compared to what they deserve? What is the worst possible outcome in this incident?" Take note of the answer you receive when you pose this question.

Just saying "Not a Big Deal" to yourself in an emphatic manner can lead the mind out of its exaggeration. Let's explore its application in daily life with some examples.

1. Imagine you are working on a project in your office. You aim to progress with your own ideas; however, your boss keeps interrupting with instructions and pointing out mistakes in your work. Consequently, you start feeling less confident, distressed, and disheartened. In such moments, say, "Not a Big Deal," and refocus on your work to break free from the situation. Eventually, you may realize that your concerns about your boss were unfounded, and it was merely your mind's exaggeration.

2. An elderly gentleman was suffering from memory loss. He struggled to remember where he had placed certain things and felt dejected. He started feeling depressed and wondered, "I don't understand why I fail to remember these small things. I cannot even remember simple details." Then, he started using this phrase. Whenever he forgot things, he immediately said, "Not a Big Deal, I always remember the important things on time." This shift in his mindset allowed him to enjoy his life.

Similarly, you can use the phrase "Not a Big Deal" in daily life situations. It will have a positive effect, and things that once seemed significant will appear less daunting.

You may question, "Am I running away from my problems by simply saying, 'It Doesn't matter' or 'Not a Big Deal'?"

Rather, the converse is true. This is not escapism but a smart way of directing the mind toward constructive solutions. Using the phrase "Not a Big Deal" doesn't mean neglecting the problem. Instead, you are calming your mind and stopping its incessant chatter about the issue. You are applying breaks on the mind's habit of exaggerating things and striving to perceive situations as they are. This is not escaping but involves gaining a deeper understanding and steering your thoughts in the right direction, leading to problem resolution.

Until our next session, make the most of the phrase "Not a Big Deal" to alleviate grief.

15

Meditation to Heal the Distress of the Past

In the last two sessions, you learned how to live a simple, stress-free life using mantras like "It Doesn't Matter" and "Not a Big Deal." You also witnessed their results. You were able to emerge from your worries quickly. After experimenting with these phrases with some past incidents, you experienced a reduction in your burden to some extent.

 Can you please share your experience?

Now, let's delve deeper into these two phrases through a meditation. During this meditation, you will focus on the incidents you keep alive in your mind by repeatedly thinking about them.

Please read the instructions first before practicing the meditation.

1. Sit comfortably in a quiet place and close your eyes.
2. Take a few deep breaths.
3. Recall a minor incident. For instance, you were not welcomed at someone's place and offered a drink. A vegetable vendor overcharged you. You couldn't find a taxi on time and arrived late at the office. You couldn't find your keys on time and got delayed. You expected a gift, appreciation, or sympathy but couldn't receive it. You had an argument with someone, etc.
4. Now, recall that incident and tell yourself, "It Doesn't Matter; such things do happen." If the incident comes to mind again,

repeat the phrase, "It Doesn't Matter," two to three times. This can help reduce the distress caused by the incident.

5. Now, think of another incident that causes you more grief or distress when you recall it. For example, somebody insulted you. Your children disobeyed you and did as they pleased. Your colleague took credit for your hard work without acknowledging your contribution. You had a family dispute where you were misunderstood. You suffered from an illness in the past.

    Such incidents tend to linger in our mind for a long time or get triggered when the topic arises, causing distress. For these incidents, tell yourself, "Not a Big Deal."

6. Now, recall that incident. As you remember it, you may feel the same distress as before. Immediately tell yourself, "Not a Big Deal." Repeat this exercise 2 to 3 times, and you will notice a reduction in the intensity of distress. Don't be disheartened if it does not happen in the first attempt. Keep recalling the incident and saying, "Not a Big Deal." Eventually, when you remember that incident, you will automatically respond, "Not a Big deal," and feel relieved from the grief and pain caused by it.

7. Sit in silence for some time. Then, open your eyes with a feeling of gratitude.

Hope you have understood how to practice this meditation. Now, put this book aside and practice it with a couple of other incidents. You may set a timer for 5 to 10 minutes for this meditation.

How do you feel after practicing this meditation?

Whenever you practice this meditation in the future, feel free to include more than two incidents if time permits.

16

Living in the Present

If this song rings in your heart, then sing along –

Shed the past's burden, its words are mere dust in the wind.

In this fresh dawn, we inscribe an inspiring tale, hand in hand.

What a song of fortitude! But can the burden of the past indeed be shed so easily?

No! You might ask how we could let go, for those very memories are our life support, holding onto which we are alive today. Otherwise, life is so arduous, filled with trials and tribulations, that we won't feel like living.

Is this true with you, too?   ☐ Yes / ☐ No

Do you struggle to live in the present?   ☐ Yes / ☐ No

Don't you think you are repeating similar phrases today that you used to in the past events? In the past, you used to say something like, "Life is full of difficulties. When will this ordeal end?" The words may not necessarily be the same, but the underlying message is. You are still facing the same challenges and struggles today as you used to. What was once your present has become your past now and your present will soon become your past. Thus, there is hardly any change in the present circumstances, but time has moved on.

If you carefully reflect, you have never really lived in the present. You kept aspiring to live life and did not realize when the present slipped out of your hands and vanished like the past. You spent most of the time in your present reminiscing about the past or dreaming about the future.

This does not mean that it is your fault, nor are you responsible for it. And it is not that you deliberately chose to live like that. We all are so entangled in the fast-paced nature of life that we fail to recognize when the day turns to night and today becomes tomorrow; we lose track of time. For the entire day, we are engrossed in the thoughts of the past and the future. Sometimes, our thoughts run in one direction and sometimes in another. Without much thinking and understanding, we become attached to them and heedlessly cling to the past or chase after the future.

Very few people know the art of focusing their thoughts in the right direction. Due to the lack of direction, thoughts drive us helter-skelter in all directions and make us do things that we won't otherwise do with a clear and directed mind. Consequently, we regret our past mistakes and get consumed by worries about the future. In this process, we lose the beautiful moment of the present. The leading cause of depression is the inability to live in the present.

Let's understand the importance of living in the present with the help of an analogy.

There was a unique dense forest where every tree bore a number. Within this forest existed a town where every resident had a special ball, with which they were supposed to play and live their life. So, they were engaged in playing with the balls. They would fall down and get up in between to resume playing with the ball.

Each ball had a number concealed on its surface that would gradually reveal itself as its surface wore down through continuous play. Once the number was exposed, it was essential for the resident to locate the tree bearing the corresponding number.

Beneath that tree, a treasure trove of love, joy, peace, awareness, prosperity, health, and good relationships awaited them. Thus, revealing the number was crucial for bringing these positive elements into their life.

However, people often became engrossed in doing everything else except playing with the ball. They would discuss their frustrations from the game and strategize for the next game. As a result, they would miss out on playing with the ball and uncovering the number. Moreover, the balls also contained seeds that needed to be released. As they played, cracks would develop on the worn-out surface of the balls, causing the seeds to fall onto the ground. It became evident that the more they would play with the ball, the faster the number would be revealed, and they would become free from the seeds by releasing them.

 What did you understand from this analogy?

In this analogy, the forest represents our life and the ball represents the present moment. As we traverse through life, it is essential to stay in the present moment, living it fully and enjoying it as much as we can. The "playing with the ball" implies happily performing activities in the present moment, which must be constant and uninterrupted. The number on the tree symbolizes the beautiful future that awaits us. Joyfully engaging in the present helps shape our future beautifully.

The seeds within the ball represent the past, with memories and history hidden in the present, emerging during incidents. Letting go of these memories is key to freeing ourselves and creating a beautiful future. Both these transformations happen only in the present.

Understanding the importance of remaining in the present moment is essential for reaping the fruits of health, love, and happiness in the future. Each day, we should celebrate new experiences and encounters. Just as victory and defeat are part of a game, the game of life is filled with a mix of pleasant and unpleasant experiences. If past experiences are negative, you may feel burdened with the regrets of the past and the worries of the future, leading to depression. You must learn to shed the weight of the past and focus on the present to genuinely savor new experiences. The following two techniques can help you steer clear of the pitfalls of negative thoughts and live in the present.

1. Focus on your breath

When you are overwhelmed with thoughts of disappointment or sorrow, start focusing on your breath. This will bring you into the present moment. Our breathing pace mirrors fluctuations in our thoughts and feelings. For example, when you are outraged, you start breathing rapidly, your body temperature rises, and your heart rate also increases. Conversely, when you are disappointed, your breath slows down, making it difficult to breathe. While everyone's experiences vary, whenever this happens, take some deep breaths immediately to restore a normal breathing pattern. It is not necessary to regulate your breathing; rather, you only need to observe the breathing as it is, and it will gradually normalize.

2. Become alert and instruct yourself loudly

If you find your thoughts drifting in the past or future while working in the present, immediately verbalize what you are doing and why. For instance, suppose you are busy working on your laptop, and thoughts of the past intrude. Now, although you seem to be working on the computer, your mind is preoccupied with the thoughts of the past. At such times, loudly remind yourself, "I must complete this work on time. Otherwise, it may impact my career." Clearly state why you are performing that activity.

When you verbalize this way, your mind will promptly shift its focus from the entangled thoughts to the present task. This will serve as a standing instruction for your mind, allowing you to engage in your current work with full awareness.

Both techniques may appear simple, but they will help you remain alert in the present. Until we reconvene in the next session, keep practicing these techniques and enjoy the bliss of being in the present.

17

Bother Then, when 'Then' Becomes Now

Hope you were able to practice the techniques learned in our previous session to remain in the present. In this session, let's delve into future worries.

Take a moment to think about the worries or anxieties that weigh on your mind and make you feel depressed. They could be concerns about your work, relationships, or fulfillment of your dreams. Do you ever find yourself thinking, "If this particular thing happens, I shall act in this manner. But what if things don't go as planned?" and so on?

 What kind of negative thoughts about the future make you feel depressed?

While it is normal to have occasional thoughts about the future that bother you, persistent worry and anxiety can lead to depression. Repeatedly dwelling on a subject or obsessing over small matters for hours is a sign of mental stress.

 How often and for how long do you think about the future every day? For example, do these thoughts cross your mind four times a day or occupy your mind for about half an hour a day?

If you spend around an hour thinking about the future solely for planning purposes, that is acceptable because planning is necessary. However, if you find yourself obsessing over the future for hours or if such thoughts make you worried or upset, it is crucial to address this habit and improve your understanding.

Are you prepared to work on this? ☐ Yes / ☐ No

Your answer will surely be "Yes." To deal with such situations, you can make use of a simple sentence that can serve as a mantra for you - **"Bother then, when 'then' becomes now."**

 Please read this mantra aloud a few times: "Bother then, when 'then' becomes now."

This means we will bother about the future only when it becomes the present. Let's not fret about the future and miss out on the crucial present moment. For now, let's stay in the present and make the most of it. This approach is essential to be at peace and in joy.

It takes just a fraction of a second for a thought to pop up in our mind and achieve its objective successfully, yet we spend hours mulling over it. We need to stop this habit.

For instance, someone fails to pay their credit card bill on time due to insufficient funds. They may worry, "What will happen now? Will my card be blocked? If it doesn't get activated on time, how will I make my future purchases?" If a shortage of funds is a major concern for them and they dwell on this issue for an extended period, it can lead to anxiety and distress. The more they dwell on it, the more they feel depressed. In such cases, it becomes imperative to break this habit of excessive thinking. Applying this mantra can help reduce their excessive thinking and refocus on the present moment, thus enabling them to take the necessary action.

Let us explore how to effectively apply this mantra using some examples.

1. Suppose someone calls you a fool and you immediately think, "I will get back at them tomorrow! They will regret calling me names!" At such times, remember the mantra, "Bother then, when 'then' becomes now." Take a step back and tell yourself, "Let's see what happens when we meet tomorrow." By doing so, you can quickly reorient yourself to the present moment.

2. Many students often find themselves pondering about the future, "Will I get a good job after my studies? Will I find a suitable life partner? Will I get an opportunity to go abroad? Will my parents find a suitable successor in me, and if they do, will I live up to their expectations? What does the future hold for my children?"

As they engage in this kind of thinking, it breeds fear, worry, and anxiety, ultimately affecting their current studies. Therefore, armed with the understanding of the mantra "Bother then, when 'then' becomes now," they need to determine how many years ahead they should think. Ideally, they should think about their studies now and consider securing a job only after completing their studies. Otherwise, prolonged contemplation about distant possibilities unnecessarily consumes their valuable time. Hence, they need to learn to shorten this time, which will, in turn, minimize the potential for disappointment.

Now, apply this understanding to an incident in your own life. Consider the future thoughts you often get entangled with and how you can apply this mantra to the particular situation.

Great! Now, you understand how to use this mantra effectively. If we carefully examine, our overthinking does not make a big difference. Even if problems are there, they tend to get resolved with time. If we look back on life, we will realize that the things we once worried about, which seemed like significant problems, are no longer there. They are either resolved or no longer relevant.

Let's consider a businessman named Harish who had to pay his employees their salaries. Every time, he would fall short of money. Although he knew that he would get the money from various sources, he would be worried about whether he would receive the money or not. Every time, he would manage to pay their salaries on time, yet every month, he would be worried about their salaries. This cycle continued for years. The moment of relief, which would bring him peace, was certain to come, yet he would remain engulfed in worries throughout the day.

Similarly, whenever we face problems, we feel distressed. In such moments, we must remind ourselves that these problems are temporary; they will pass with time. There is no need to be so upset by repeatedly thinking about them. Instead, embrace the mantra, "Bother then, when 'then' becomes now."

 Reflect on your life and see whether the problems you faced some years ago persist or have ended. How do you perceive them today?

Do they trouble you in the same way as they did previously?

☐ Yes / ☐ No

There are many examples that show that when a problem comes, the solutions to the problem are also given. We all have had such experiences and will continue to have them even in the future. Hence, it is time to have faith in nature and understand, "Bother then, when 'then' becomes now. Let us cross the bridge when we come to it. When a problem arises, only then we will think about it. Let's live a worry-free life with happiness."

Until the next session, use this mantra thoroughly so that you will witness its miracles and enjoy the present moment.

18

Steering Clear of Past Hurts

We all have days when our spirits may dip. How are you feeling today? Is everything alright?

 Can you recall an incident in which someone's words deeply hurt you?

Today, we will discuss how to safeguard ourselves from being emotionally hurt by others.

At times, we feel deeply hurt by others' words. Even seemingly trivial conversations can trigger these feelings. Sometimes, a simple sentence can carry a weight that profoundly saddens us. We may feel insulted or accused by others.

Sometimes, we become so attached to certain words or phrases that whenever we hear them, they elicit pain, whether knowingly or unknowingly. We feel sad every time we recall them. We may even believe that the other person intentionally used those words to hurt us. However, they may have spoken those words unintentionally, without realizing that they have hurt us. As a result, we continue to blame them for our emotional distress.

This is because people come from diverse backgrounds and experiences, and different words hold varying degrees of emotional weight for different people. For example, someone who has experienced childhood obesity might have a stronger emotional reaction to weight-related comments than someone who hasn't. However, it is essential to recognize that those who are commenting may not have intended to hurt us; they may simply be unaware that the word or topic is a sensitive trigger for us.

To illustrate this point, let's consider the concept of the generation gap, which often leads to ideological differences between younger and older family members.

A disagreement arose between a father and a son over a trivial matter. It aggravated to the point where the father asked the son to leave the house. The son, being very sensitive, was deeply hurt by his father's words. He felt depressed for many days. Eventually, misunderstandings were cleared, and everything returned to normal. However, even after many years, whenever the son recalled that incident, he felt nervous. Unknowingly, he was hurting himself by remembering that incident.

Even after many years have passed, if someone's words or actions still hurt us, it means that we are hurting ourselves, and no one else is responsible for it.

Reflect on your own life. Do you find any words, phrases, or incidents that still bother you even after a considerable period has passed?

☐ Yes / ☐ No

Have you been blaming others for these emotions and considering someone else the cause of your depression? ☐ Yes / ☐ No

One can spend their entire life in this misunderstanding that the cause of their distress lies with other people and their behavior. However, the converse is true. Regardless of others' behavior, as long as we do not allow their words or behavior to affect us emotionally, they cannot overpower us.

However, we commit the mistake of associating ourselves with those words and hurting ourselves. Instead of raising our awareness, we expect others to consider our feelings because we feel they purposely hurt us. We feel more disappointed when they don't meet our expectations.

You might have noticed how seemingly insignificant incidents can prick like a needle, triggering negative emotions and causing distress. For example, when a close relative invited all your family members except you to a function, it was hurtful. It can be disheartening to eagerly await joining your friends on a picnic, only to realize they went without informing you. You may feel isolated when all your colleagues are working on a project, but you are not informed about it. Your partner's frequent friendly banter with a coworker might lead to feelings of jealousy and insecurity. You may feel deflated and hurt when your colleague was appreciated for their work, but you were ignored. Likewise, negative feelings have accumulated within us due to so many incidents, which can later be triggered by seemingly insignificant events or actions, causing distress.

All these words, incidents, and situations are like unwanted guests or strangers. Just as you would not let strangers into your home and would talk to them from outside, you must say goodbye to these painful, pricking words and situations from a distance.

Would you like to free yourself from such words and hurtful feelings that come uninvited and catch you off guard?   ☐ Yes / ☐ No

Would you like to disregard the pain they inflict?   ☐ Yes / ☐ No

By saying "Yes," you grant yourself freedom from the burden of hurtful emotions.

Incidents will continue to happen in life, but it is our choice whether to free ourselves from the hurt or allow ourselves to be hurt. To achieve this, we need to take three crucial steps:

1. Be Alert

You might have experienced that you feel hurt when interacting with some people, hearing specific words, or remembering certain events. First, become alert of where and when you feel hurt, identifying which words and incidents cause you pain.

To maintain an unhurt state, repeatedly affirm to yourself, "I love myself. I stand for love. No matter how much anyone hurts me, I choose to live with love and joy so that I remain unhurt."

2. Make a choice

During such times, while remaining alert, make a conscious choice whether you want to stay happy or sad. Thus, whenever you feel hurt, take a moment to introspect and ask yourself, "How long do I choose to remain in this hurtful state?" Then, patiently wait for the answer.

3. Follow the answer

If you choose to be sad for one or two hours, endure the pain for that long but remind yourself that you are doing it out of choice. You may set an alarm for that duration. However, do not allow yourself to be sad for even a minute after the alarm goes off. Immediately shift your focus away from the incident using any of the techniques learned in the earlier sessions to get out of sorrow.

It is up to you whether you allow yourself to be hurt or not. If you do not want to be hurt, no power in the world can hurt you. Therefore, decide what you truly want in life.

After this session, take some time to reflect and write down the incidents and words that have hurt you and how you would change your response having learned the new steps in this session.

We will reconvene in the next session. Thank you.

19

Dealing With Emotions

Welcome to today's session.

Are you currently experiencing feelings of depression?

☐ Yes / ☐ No

If not, please recall a past incident when you felt depressed. Do you feel depressed now by remembering it? ☐ Yes / ☐ No

Whether you felt depressed earlier or after recalling it now, please close your eyes and mentally navigate through your body to notice the sensations in each part of your body. Are you feeling a tingle in the spine, heaviness in the shoulders, a choked sensation in the throat, tightness in the chest or forehead, discomfort in the stomach, rapid heartbeats or breathing, or heat in the ears? Spend five minutes observing these sensations.

🎤 Describe precisely what you are currently experiencing in each part of your body. It could be a physical pain or discomfort.

Great! Have you noticed any change in your emotions, sensations, or thoughts after witnessing your body sensations? ☐ Yes / ☐ No

If not, please repeat this simple exercise because it has the power to alleviate your negative emotions.

Have you ever found yourself or someone you know saying, "I don't know why, but my mind has been restless all day. I woke up feeling refreshed, but suddenly, my mood took a downturn. I don't feel like engaging in anything or talking to anyone."

 Please write about the moments when you feel sad, and life seems burdensome and meaningless.

Agreed! At times, everyone goes through experiences where they feel sad and lack the motivation for any activity.

Would you like to know why this happens?   ☐ Yes / ☐ No

We go through many negative incidents from childhood, the thoughts of which accumulate in our minds. Some leave a lasting imprint on our minds, and even when we want to move on, they linger in our consciousness. These memories or related triggers can resurface unexpectedly, causing mental distress.

For instance, some individuals feel stressed during exam periods, such as the months of April and May. Even after they have passed their exams, the feeling of stress is triggered during these months because the brain has stored the memory of exam-related anxiety and associated it with these months. When April and May come around, the brain automatically retrieves the memory, rekindling the same feelings of stress.

Similarly, some people experience negative emotions during specific seasons due to past negative experiences. Some people struggle to accept changes due to seasons or any other reasons.

Likewise, negative associations with words, colors, or festivals can profoundly impact some people. Even after many years have passed, merely hearing those words, or seeing those colors can evoke a sense of sadness within them. Sometimes, they might not even remember the childhood incident linked to these triggers, yet the emotions persist. If a song was playing at the time of their loved one's funeral, they may feel the same pain when they hear the song again even after many years.

The reasons behind these responses can vary from person to person. While we may encounter such situations from time to time, we must learn to cope with them.

What do you think? Do you also wish to confront these situations instead of avoiding them and strive to move forward with a feeling of joy?
☐ Yes / ☐ No

Now, let us understand what you need to do. Regardless of the cause of depression, do not get entangled in it; instead, confront it. How can you achieve this? By observing it with complete awareness.

Observing the feelings arising in the body

Whenever we go through any incident, whether pleasant or unpleasant, we experience various feelings and sensations within our bodies. When our thoughts are positive, we feel joy, enthusiasm, and passion. On the other hand, when our thoughts are negative, we feel disappointment, sorrow, discouragement, fatigue, and dullness.

You must have noticed that whenever your mind feels disappointed, your face droops and you feel like crying. You experience a strange silence, loneliness, and a trembling sensation throughout your body. Some people become so overwhelmed with sadness that they cannot utter a single word. They appear sick and exhausted as if all their energy has been drained. Similarly, when fear arises, they experience sweating, a rapid heartbeat, trembling, and an upset stomach. The mind becomes extremely alarmed and restless.

 Please note down your experience. Usually, what happens to you when you go through such feelings?

It is not wrong to experience these feelings. They are a natural part of being human. However, people often get stuck in them, asking themselves, "Why is this happening? Why do I feel so low? Why is my body trembling?" By repeatedly thinking this way, they become consumed by negative thoughts and emotions. However, you need to learn to observe these thoughts and feelings as they are, with detachment.

You might have observed that when you gently care for an injured part of your body with love and attention, it slowly begins to heal. However, if you ignore it, the same area gets hurt repeatedly, and the wound becomes deeper.

Similarly, attentively observe all the sensations and changes happening in your body. Without doing anything, simply acknowledge that changes are happening within the body and pay a little attention to them. Then, resume your work.

With this practice, you will notice that all the sadness accumulated in your body begins to evaporate gradually, eventually coming to an end.

Thought watching

The mind tends to exaggerate every incident. It plays a crucial role by envisaging make-believe stories and compelling us to believe in them completely. Regrettably, we often accept these stories as true and unquestioningly trust our minds. By constantly listening to the mind, we can even fall into the trap of depression but will never doubt our own thoughts.

It is akin to someone embracing a pillar and seeking help to separate from it. Passersby mock the futility of the situation. Likewise, we are also attached to our thoughts. We also long to detach ourselves from them but find it challenging. However, when we observe our thoughts with detachment, it becomes easier to let them go.

 Which thoughts can you easily let go of, and which ones prove more difficult to release?

From now on, when negative thoughts arise, do not believe them immediately. Instead, take a pause and simply observe them without reacting. How can you achieve this?

When a thought of sadness arises within you, calmly observe what kind of thoughts are arising. Notice if the feeling of despair is increasing or thoughts are piling up one after the other. Every time a thought arises, silently say "Next" and watch it pass. Avoid engaging in any conversation like, "Why did this thought arise? When will it go away? What will happen next?" Just observe the thoughts come and go. When the next thought arises, say "Next" to it again. Keep saying "Next" to every thought. After some time, the number of thoughts will reduce, and the feeling of despair will subside. Thus, by simply observing your thoughts, they will gradually subside and eventually come to an end.

Now, close your eyes for some time and observe how the thoughts gradually subside as you say "Next" to them as they surface.

Could you say "Next" to the thoughts that made you sad when you recalled them? What happened when you tried this technique?

With the new understanding gained in this session, witness the feelings of despair as they are to free yourself from them. This is an effective way to overcome sorrow. Neither suppress the feeling of despair nor vent it out on others as anger; instead, mindfully observe it with awareness. Understand that the accumulated feeling of despair has surfaced, only to be released.

Please experiment with the practices suggested here.

So far, we have learned some simple yet powerful techniques to relieve ourselves from distress. In the upcoming sessions, we will discuss some advanced techniques that will help us understand the profound secrets of spirituality. See you in the next session. Thank you.

20

The Chain of Thoughts, Feelings, and Mood

Hello! How are you feeling today?

In the previous session, we understood how to deal with emotions.

Let's start today's session with a story.

Nisha was visiting her uncle after many years. As a child, she used to frequent their house during vacations. However, when she was in college, her parents parted ways with them due to arguments over some differences over their ancestral property. Now, after many years, her uncle had invited her family.

While traveling to her uncle's town, Nisha was feeling nostalgic about the days bygone when she would play and sing with her cousins. She was overjoyed and looked forward to their reunion. On the day of her travel, she kept humming the songs the sisters used to sing together.

When they reached her uncle's house, Nisha found that her cousins had already arrived the previous day. All her cousins were working in unison, paying no heed to her presence. When she tried to strike up a conversation with some of them, they just replied curtly and ignored her. She was taken aback and felt disheartened and isolated. Later, when she was alone in the room, she wept over the stark contrast that she was facing vis-à-vis what she had enjoyed as a child. She felt as though she didn't belong there at all. She started having thoughts like, "They have all changed. They are no longer the same people who loved me. I shouldn't have come here. I was happy back home. I want to return home as soon as possible."

So, what exactly was transpiring in Nisha's mind? The sudden change in her thoughts, emotions, and mood, her sudden despondency and change of heart—how does it all connect? What do you think?

Before visiting her uncle, Nisha was overjoyed and looking forward to the visit. But when her expectations were dashed, she felt sad and disappointed. Thus, we can see that during this sequence of events, her thoughts, emotions, and mood underwent a change.

 Now, let's get to the very basics. Please share what you understand about thoughts, emotions, and mood. What are thoughts, emotions, and mood? How are they related? And how are they different?

We often discuss so many things using terms like thoughts, emotions, and mood, but we rarely think about what they really mean. Now, let's understand them in detail.

Thoughts are the mental processes that occur in our brain, triggered either internally from memory or in response to external stimuli from our surroundings, people, or events. Thereafter, they are interpreted using the language we speak within. These thought forms are associated with various feelings that have been programmed in our subconscious mind since childhood. When these feelings manifest on the body in the form of sensations, they are called emotions. Emotions can be short-lived, but they can alter our mood, which can linger for a long period. Conversely, our moods and feelings can also trigger associated thoughts.

In Nisha's case, the thought of going to her uncle's place triggered rich memories and she felt overjoyed. However, when she didn't receive the warm welcome she expected, this contradictory stimulus triggered negative thoughts within her, making her feel rejected and dejected. As her emotions and mood changed, so did her thoughts.

Thus, thoughts, emotions, and moods are interrelated. They are like the legs of a stool on which we are seated from morning till night, driving our actions and behavior. So, we need to work on our thoughts, emotions, moods, and even actions to heal depression.

In the previous sessions, we have already discussed strategies for altering our thoughts and feelings, which in turn affect our mood. You may wonder how actions can help in healing. In Nisha's case, when she started recollecting how she used to play and sing with her cousins, her rich memories from childhood sprang to life, and she started feeling happy and humming those melodies.

Here, the **"Act as if - - -"** mantra comes to your rescue. It is a deliberate attempt to do a particular action to change one's state of mind. For example, whenever your mood is low or you feel dejected, deliberately act as if you are overflowing with happiness. Your inner state will automatically change. This is also the philosophy on which laughing clubs have been started. When people get together and deliberately laugh aloud, their feelings begin to change positively. In the same way, when you feel lethargic, act as if you are the most active person. For this, you may start dancing or do some quick body stretches. You will soon feel energetic.

 Think of an example where you can practice this.

When things didn't turn out as Nisha would have liked, she was saddened. She could have grumbled, grieved over the situation, and blamed her uncle, aunt, and cousins for her entire life, making life miserable for herself. The more she would have thought over it, the more she would have sunk into the abyss of gloom.

 But is this the only choice Nisha had? Couldn't she have chosen to respond differently? Are her relatives to be fully blamed and responsible for her sorrow? What do you think?

Surely, her relatives are not to be entirely blamed or fully responsible for her sorrow. They may have behaved rudely intentionally or unintentionally just once. But to make it worse for herself, Nisha kept ruminating over the incident repeatedly, thus keeping the event alive in her mind. When one goes through such constant rumination, it becomes difficult to break the loop of thoughts and divert one's focus to something constructive. Then they need to seek professional help. But if one can break this loop right in the beginning by adopting some techniques to shift their focus and overcome the barrage of negative thoughts, one can become free from this trap.

Imagine a moving belt on which various potted plants are placed. You stand next to the moving belt and water the pot that comes before you. There are beautiful flower plants, some thorny plants, and some wild weeds. Will you water them all?

Of course, you won't. You will water only those plants that you want to grow. Similarly, based on our mood, memory, the weather, and surroundings, we are bound to have a variety of thoughts running in our mind. But it is entirely up to us which thoughts we choose to nourish with our attention. The unnecessary thoughts may repeatedly arise before us and try to suck our attention but if we don't pay them attention, they will diminish and vanish just as plants dry and wither when they are not watered.

So, if Nisha had shifted her focus to some positive thoughts, she would not have suffered as much as she did. She could have reminisced the good old rich memories and kept humming those songs to keep herself happy.

But when one feels the pangs of sorrow, one finds it difficult to choose to be happy. Even though happiness is what we all desire, why can't we always rejoice and be happy unconditionally? Why do we experience sorrow in the first place?

Contemplate these questions until we reconvene in the next session. Thank you!

21

Understanding Sorrow

Hi! Hope you were able to contemplate the real causes of sorrow.

Before we discuss the main causes of sorrow, let us consider the following examples.

- Consider a pregnant woman who goes through labor pain to give birth to her baby. She endures pain for her baby.
- A caterpillar endures pain to emerge as a butterfly. If it resists the pain, it won't enjoy the bliss of freedom of the butterfly.

Similarly, it is nature's arrangement for us to endure sorrow to unleash our hidden potential. Sorrow actually means "so-called" or "perceived" sorrow because what we regard as sorrow is actually not sorrow but a deception. It is an illusion like the mirage in the desert. What we regard as sorrow is actually an invitation for growth. It comes to make us mentally tough and mature. Thus, "so-called" sorrow serves as the driving force that strengthens our quest for true happiness. If viewed from the right perspective, sorrow is actually an opportunity for growth.

We grieve because we resist the feeling of sorrow by considering it real and permanent. The moment we stop resisting sorrow and allow it to play out, we find that it is a temporary wave that comes and goes.

Since childhood, we have had many experiences. Our brain labels them as good or bad and stores them in our memory. Whenever similar incidents happen, our brain gives programmed responses, and we experience happiness or sorrow.

To add to this, we get caught up in this illusion of sorrow because it is a common mistake that we see everyone committing. When everyone commits the same mistake, it doesn't seem like a mistake; it becomes the norm. Everyone believes that we must brood over a sorrowful event and rejoice over a happy event.

Imagine – from childhood, if we had grown up seeing everyone around us celebrate, dance, and make merry when a sorrowful event occurs, how would we regard sorrow?

We all have been living in a trance of mass hypnosis, where we have been made to believe that problems and challenges are bad and should not occur. We have believed that events that do not align with our expectations should not occur and should be resisted. It is a deep illusion.

When we develop an unshakable conviction about the illusory nature of sorrow, we can choose to be happy in the face of sorrow. Whenever we encounter sorrow, we will laugh.

The body may undergo physical pain, which cannot be avoided. But the mental distress that we suffer due to that pain is our choice. We must remember that we have a choice in every moment of our life. We can embrace pain as an opportunity to experience this freedom of choice.

We all feel natural and peaceful when we are happy. However, when we drift away from this peaceful state, we feel sad. We hold the belief that happiness is good and sorrow is bad. Hence, our mind gets attached to happiness and tries to hold onto it while it resists sorrow and struggles to avoid it.

Thus, life offers a mixed bag of events that we either embrace or resist, depending on our past conditioning. Accordingly, we experience happiness and sorrow. If this is how life is, then considering the grand scheme of life, what is the role of sorrow in life? Can you share your thoughts on this?

Everything happens in life spontaneously as part of the divine plan. However, when our mind resists it, we experience sorrow. Sorrow is like the red indicator shown on the fuel gauge when the vehicle is short of fuel. Sorrow is an indication from nature that we have drifted away from our peaceful, happy state; it only means we need to restore our happy state. But instead of restoring it, we start brooding over sorrow, imagining that it is permanent, thus aggravating it further.

Whenever we feel sorrow, we can practice Witnessing meditation to alter our thoughts, emotions, and mood, in turn enabling us to respond differently. We can sit for a few minutes with closed eyes and observe the negative feelings that arise within.

There are five key aspects to this observation:

1. Equanimity: We need to observe our feelings with equanimity, without labeling them as good or bad. Just watch them arise and pass, knowing that they are neither positive nor negative, neither good nor bad.

2. Evenness: They may seem like heavy feelings of the order of 50 kilograms in severity. But we can observe them, knowing that they are neither 50 kilograms nor 5 grams. Observe every feeling with such evenness.

3. Understanding: Watch the emotions with the understanding that they are temporary. They have appeared only to stay for some time and then vanish. Knowing this, there is no need to resist them.

4. Inner cleansing: Know that the emotions were already pent up within you. The external trigger – whether it was a person or some event – only served as a hook to evoke and weed them out so that you can achieve inner cleansing and become free from them.

5. Awareness: Watch the feelings that arise with the awareness that they are not happening with you; rather they are happening inside the body. The higher this awareness, the more easily feelings dissolve in the ocean of awareness.

When the Buddha experienced sorrow, he was caught up with profound questions about his own existence and embarked on the journey of liberation from sorrow. On attaining the state of Enlightenment, he worked with the mission of eradicating sorrow in human life. Thus, sorrow became a blessing in disguise for him.

Sorrow can become a stepping-stone in our life to progress toward our goal, provided we perceive it with the right understanding and witness it with awareness and equanimity.

Let's understand some more benefits of sorrow.

- Sorrow breaks our stupor of mechanical living and can motivate us to experiment with something new.
- Sorrow pushes us to leave the comfort zone of depending on others for our happiness and subjecting ourselves to the constant flux of joy and sorrow. It embarks us on the mission of attaining the everlasting state of unconditional bliss that transcends joy and sorrow.
- Sorrow helps us heal the wounds caused by injured memories.
- Sorrow helps us return to our true essence and attain Self-realization – the ultimate purpose of human life.

Until our next session, list down the sorrowful events of your life and contemplate how you can convert them into ladders for growth. Thank you!

PART 3

SPIRITUAL GROWTH AND EMPOWERMENT

22

The Voice of Faith

Happy Thoughts! Welcome to this session.

Were you taken aback by the phrase "Happy Thoughts?" It might be a new greeting for you. Today, we are going to learn a significant life lesson. So, let's kick off our session in a new style, with new words.

 Please share your initial thoughts after hearing the greeting "Happy Thoughts."

"Happy Thoughts" is more than just a phrase. It is a reminder to always have happy thoughts. Happy thoughts inspire us to keep hope and faith alive in our lives. In today's discussion, our focus will revolve around these essential themes of "Hope" and "Faith."

Hope is the tiny ray of light that penetrates through the darkness of negativity. When overwhelmed with negativity, hope is the fuel that inspires us to keep going. Hope is the strength to persevere in the face of adversity. In challenging times, when hope wanes, problems tend to linger. Whereas, when faith guides our thoughts, we firmly believe that everything can be resolved; no external force can shake us. Let's understand this with the help of a compelling real-life story.

Vijender Singh, a resident of Ajmer, India, used to work with a travel agency. In 2013, his wife, Leela, insisted they go on a pilgrimage to the *Char Dham* in Northern India. The travel agency had a scheduled tour to Kedarnath, a Hindu pilgrimage site nestled in the picturesque Himalayan mountains in India. It is home to a revered Lord Shiva temple. They reached Kedarnath and checked into a lodge. While Vijender went about his work, Leela stayed back at the lodge. On that fateful day, the raging waters of the devastating flood in Uttarakhand inundated Kedarnath, causing total chaos in the region.

In a harrowing struggle for survival, Vijender battled against overwhelming odds. When the floodwaters finally receded, he returned to the lodge. To his dismay, the entire area had been swept away by the merciless floods in the landslide, leaving no trace of his beloved wife. Undeterred, he tirelessly searched for days on end. Even in her absence, Vijender's resolute mantra remained unchanged: "Leela is alive." While his children had reluctantly come to terms with their mother's presumed demise, Vijender did not give up.

In contrast to those who accepted government monetary compensation, Vijender clung steadfastly to hope and refused to take the compensation. Instead, he searched for her from town to town, showing her picture to everyone he met. After canvassing over a thousand villages, his unwavering faith bore fruit on January 27, 2015. Upon glimpsing Leela's picture, a passerby identified her as a bewildered woman wandering in his village, completely lost and disoriented. Without wasting time, Vijender traveled with the stranger to his village and was finally reunited with his beloved wife. His joy knew no bounds as he held her once more.

Vijender's story is a testament to the formidable strength of unwavering hope. Amidst daunting challenges, he clung resolutely to the hope that his wife was alive and that he would find her. His unshakable faith was ultimately rewarded. His remarkable hope and infallible faith remained undeterred, and even the forces of the universe rallied behind him to make it happen. If one believes in oneself, the universe also bends to one's will.

Therefore, one should hold onto hope until the last moment. Doctors never give up on hope. They do everything they can until the last moment to save a patient's life.

Have you experienced a situation where you maintained hope throughout, and eventually, everything turned out fine? ☐ Yes / ☐ No

Hope and Faith are treasures that nothing can take away from us, no matter how much trouble we face. Sometimes, people are on the brink of achieving their goals but falter in their hope. Later, they often regret it. Merely a step away from their destination, their faith wavers, convincing them they won't reach their goal. Therefore, it is best never to lose hope; it is wiser always to give it one last try.

On a general note, how long do you remain hopeful? Can you remember what happened when you continued to be hopeful? Are you the type to persist despite setbacks, or do you tend to give up after a few attempts?

Along with hope, faith is equally important, for it possesses the extraordinary ability to turn the seemingly impossible into possible.

The cure for every incurable disease lies within us! The remedy to our woes and sorrows exists within us. We only need to acquaint ourselves with the remedy and work toward liberating ourselves. But how can we achieve this?

When we place our faith in God or the higher power that bears and nurtures the universe, we regard that as the most powerful entity. We seek refuge in this power to help us achieve our aspirations or pull us out of the emotional doldrums. Those who have this faith, pray to God, visit temples, shrines, or holy places, and firmly believe that God will grant their prayers. Very often, this faith indeed comes to fruition, and people manage to achieve what they desire; they emerge out of the storm of negativity.

Although faith in God is a higher form of faith, it is not the pinnacle of faith. Be it faith in God or faith in our friends or relatives, such faith assumes that we are this limited individual being. If we remain stuck with this limited identity, we can express faith only to the extent that it fulfills the needs and desires of this limited identity that we are stuck to.

And this brings about limited results. We remain engulfed in the cycle of pain and pleasure.

The purpose of human life is far grander. Though it may not seem obvious or believable, the pain and suffering we experience are stepping stones to a higher life where we attain the height of faith, happiness, freedom, love, and peace.

This is like an ocean taking the form of a wave that emerges from the ocean and dissolves into the ocean. Since the wave has emerged from the ocean, it has no individual existence without the ocean. Each wave is the ocean itself; it is not something separate from the ocean. If you observe a droplet of the wave under the microscope, you will find that it is nothing but the same water as the ocean; the properties of the droplet are exactly the same as the ocean. It is just that the ocean has given rise to many droplets of itself.

So, is the wave separate from the ocean? Is the wave separate from the remaining waves? Not at all! Though they are different expressions of the same ocean, they are connected at a deep level. They intermingle and share the same essence.

In the same way, God, the supreme power, created this universe where God experiences and expresses through each and every being. We all are connected with each other through our underlying essence and can never be separate. God is enacting through each of us in a beautiful orchestra that may not be evident at first. Through this orchestra, God wishes to experience love, joy, peace, and creativity.

Thus, whenever you experience self-pity and associated low feelings, ask yourself, "How does God see me? Helpless? Worthless? A low-profile or inferior person? Ill?" Of course not! God never sees anyone this way. Instead, God has a grander view of us; He has a divine plan brimming with love, joy, peace, and abundance working for us.

Then why do we experience negative emotions? The negative emotions serve as a springboard to jump higher; it is a push from God to break the limitations of the mind and fly high. Otherwise, a person stuck in his comfort zone does not make an effort by himself to take the leap of faith until nature pushes him through these negative feelings. When he gets tired of negative feelings, he decides to break through self-imposed limitations and progress.

In the future, when faced with unfamiliar or challenging situations, shift your focus away from the situation and start repeatedly affirming what God wants to experience through you. Here are some example affirmations for your reference.

- Whatever is true for God is true for me, too.
- God has made me in His image to experience and express pure love, joy, and peace. I am the Source of love, joy, and peace.
- I am a grand expression of God. My true nature is unlimited, all-knowing, and all-pervading.
- God has created my body as His vehicle. My body is whole and perfect. Let this body serve in the expression of supreme consciousness.
- The Universe is complete, and so am I.
- I am fortunate because I have unwavering faith in God. God is with me every moment.
- Nature assists me in tackling situations.
- My body and mind can fulfill my mission on Earth. I am in a state of heightened consciousness.
- With faith, even the impossible is becoming possible.
- I am healthy, happy, and liberated. I am free from all constraints.
- I have unwavering faith in my spiritual mentor.
- I have full faith that my life is filled with divine light.
- My body is counted among the healthy and trustworthy ones.

- The supreme power that takes care, nourishes, and sustains every living creature under the ocean is also taking care of me. I am assured of my well-being.
- I am God's loved creation. No evil can ever touch me.

The above affirmations serve as a reference. You can create and repeat similar affirmations in your own words. Repeat any of the above affirmations with hope and full faith. Express your gratitude to God once you have finished repeating them.

How do you feel after repeating the affirmations?

Initially, you may doubt the outcome of repeating these affirmations. However, hold onto hope and keep repeating these words with faith. If the mind rejects the thought, you can tell your mind, "I am not subscribing to this thought, but am only using this thought for my benefit." Soon, you will witness tangible results, further reinforcing your faith.

Hope this session has instilled confidence in you that depression is reversible. It can be easily cured. Strengthen your faith to such an extent that every word you speak serves as medicine for you.

Always remember that every positive or negative word ushers its own effect. In ancient times, people's curses and blessings held power. Hence, always use positive words. Until our next session, continue repeating the positive affirmations of your choice.

23

The Drama of Life

Happy Thoughts! Welcome to today's session.

Before we move on to today's profound topic, please share your experiences of repeating positive affirmations. Were you able to repeat the positive affirmations with faith? ☐ Yes / ☐ No

 How was your experience?

Let's start today's topic with an intriguing story that draws parallels to the story of our life.

Imagine a movie in which the protagonist goes through ups and downs, experiencing the highs and lows of life. He keeps suffering in the rollercoaster ride of his life. He prays for freedom from this chaotic existence, wishing it would stop and hoping life would be simple and peaceful.

In this mysterious movie, the writer-director enters the story as a character who plays a spiritual guide. The protagonist meets him and shares the sorry state that his life has become.

The guide says, "Everything that you are going through is perfect as per the script I have written. You are getting upset because you don't know how it is working behind the scenes. All you need to realize is that the scenes and dialogues in your story are of my making. You just need to agree to flow with the script. There is no need to wait for the ups and downs to vanish and a straight line to emerge."

The protagonist cannot digest what he hears and protests, "I cannot believe what you are saying. What kind of existence is this if this story is just as per your script?"

The guide smiles, "Even these lines you speak are written in the script! You speak these lines because you do not yet know the truth. Your real identity is not confined to this character in the story. You actually exist outside this movie. Whether the story is a comedy or a tragedy, the real "you" remains untouched by it. Whether the scene in the story shows the burning embers of a fire or the raging water currents of a flood, you never get burned or drenched, just like the screen on which the movie is projected remains untouched and indifferent."

Still feeling lost, the protagonist asks, "Can you please elaborate further?"

The guide elaborates, "To understand what I said, start observing your thoughts and body with detachment. Notice your thoughts and feelings as if they do not belong to you but rather to your body."

The protagonist states, "I still do not understand this."

The guide asks, "Have you ever seen a puppet show? They play different characters in the drama. How do those puppets dance in different ways?"

The protagonist replies, "They dance according to how the puppeteer controls the strings. They lack desires of their own about how to dance."

The guide exclaims, "Exactly! This world is also a show where your body is playing a part. Someone is pulling the strings, just like in a puppet show. You have a misconception that you are the character you portray and this is your life story. However, the truth is that it is not your story. The story is written by the puppeteer – the Real Self, God, Ishwar, Allah, or whatever name you want to call it. He directs this body to act. You are distinct from the body. The body experiences feelings, sensations, and thoughts. The body is just your companion. You are not the body but distinct from it."

The protagonist affirms, "Now I understand. It means that whatever happens to me is happening at the level of the body. My Real Self and the body are distinct. I should consider the body as my companion. Whatever sorrow, difficulties, and emotions happen within the body should be seen as if they are happening to my companion."

The guide concurs, "Now you have got it right. Just as you express sympathy for your friends but do not get attached to their grief, in the same way, you should only observe the sensations and feelings arising in your body. No need to get attached to them. No need to be saddened when there are painful sensations in the body. With this approach, the problem will be easily and quickly resolved. So, you need to step out of the story."

The protagonist asks the guide, "How do I step out of the story?"

"Start watching the story from a distance. Watch your character's story being played out. Observe how your character thinks, feels, speaks, behaves, and reacts to the plots and other characters of the story. As you keep observing from a distance, you will develop detachment from the fluctuations of the story and become increasingly aware of your presence outside the story."

 This profound narrative offers many shifts of perspective to us. You may want to draw parallels to your life and write down your insights.

What we assume as "My story" is actually happening in our body-mind. We are a witness to whatever happens with the body and mind. As the body and mind are always present with us, we assume that "I am this body" or "I am this mind." Hence, whatever happens to the body or mind seems to happen to us.

Consider the following sentences that are commonly spoken: "My head started paining when I went to the office. I was feeling low when my headache increased. I then thought of visiting the doctor to find a remedy."

When you say, "I went to the office", the word "I" refers to the body. You keep saying many such things during the day by assuming you are this body. For instance, "I had food, I climbed the stairs, I held the box," etc.

The same sentence also says, "My head started paining." Now, to whom does "My" refer? If you were to use the earlier identification with the body, you would say, "I started paining."

When you say, "My head started paining," you assume you are the owner of your body. It is only when you assume yourself separate from your body that you say, "My head." Thus, the reference for "I" has shifted from being the body to being the owner of the body!

When you say, "I was feeling low," the "I" here refers to the mind. The body cannot feel low. The mind feels low just as it also feels elated or angry.

"I thought of visiting the doctor." In this instance, you assume yourself to be the intellect. The reference shifts from the mind to the intellect.

This example demonstrates how the "I" keeps shifting in just three sentences. On deeper reflection, you will find countless identities of "I" that keep arising from time to time. Due to the illusion of continuity, you believe it to be the same "I." The real "I," which you truly are, remains in the dark. Your true nature never shines forth as it is eclipsed by all these false identities.

With this knowledge, you can enjoy the story by being its spectator. You can observe the various thoughts, feelings, and body sensations that arise during the day with detachment, knowing that it is happening in the body, not with you.

Whenever you find that you are getting pulled into the story, you can remind yourself by asking, "Exactly what is happening? And to whom is it happening?" If the mind says, "It is happening to me," enquire, "Who is this 'me'?" This will lead you out of the story to freedom.

Self-observation meditation

The practice of self-observation can help you notice how the state of the mind keeps changing in every situation. You begin to understand that the real cause of sorrow is the changing state of the mind, and you remain detached and peaceful outside the story.

Observe your mind in every event or situation. For this, every hour, close your eyes and be seated in a comfortable posture for 2 to 3 minutes, and ask yourself, "What is the present state of my mind?"

To answer this question, you need to narrate your present state of mind. You can consider the states from A to L:

- **A**nger: See whether the mind is angry with others, the ongoing situation, or even yourself.
- **B**oredom: Is the mind feeling dejected or lacks interest in what is going on?
- **C**onfusion: Is the mind confused or unable to understand something even after several attempts?
- **D**epression: See whether the mind is feeling distressed or agitated with or without any reason.
- **E**go: Is there a feeling of pride or arrogance? Notice whether the mind craves praise or takes credit for something that has happened.
- **F**ear: Identify if there is fear that something untoward or undesirable may happen.
- **G**uilt: See whether the mind is indulging in feelings of regret or self-blame.
- **H**appiness: Is the mind happy in the present situation?
- **I**ll-will: Is the mind entertaining any feelings of harm to others?

- **J**ealousy: See whether the mind is envious or resentful. Is it restless with the thought, "I do not have what others have?"
- **K**indness: Does the mind feel like helping or caring for others out of sympathy or compassion?
- **L**aziness: See whether the mind is feeling dull or lethargic.

Thus, you need to observe whether the mind is either angry, bored, confused, depressed, egoistic, fearful, feeling guilty, happy, feeling ill-will, jealous, kind, or lazy.

After every hour when the mind is observed with awareness, you will clearly see how the mind changes its state from time to time. After some days of consistent practice, you will realize that the desires of the mind are continuously changing. Restlessness is the nature of the mind. The untrained mind cannot remain in a steady state for long.

This hourly self-observation will lead to miracles. Soon, you will begin to understand, not just intellectually but through your own experience, that the mind is an illusion. If this is how the mind is, then why should we trust it? This knowledge will dawn on you.

Then, if the mind is upset, you will clearly distinguish that you are not upset. All these states are with the mind, not with you. Then, no thought of happiness or sorrow can displace you from your peace.

Even during times of distress, you can remain calm by reminding yourself, "This stress is with my mind and body, not with me." You will understand that this stress has appeared to get some work done through the body, just like tension before exams is necessary for a student to motivate him to study.

Now, keep this book aside. Sit in a comfortable posture and close your eyes for 5 minutes. Ask yourself, "How has the state of my mind been in the last hour?"

Jot down how you feel after completing this practice.

Incorporate this meditation as a part of your daily routine. See you in the next session.

24

Witnessing the Chattering Mind

How are you feeling today? Were you able to practice the self-observation that we discussed in the previous session? ☐ Yes / ☐ No

We have understood how we are deeply connected with everything in consciousness. We exist in God just as every wave exists within the ocean. The real purpose of life is to discover our connectedness with our divine essence and live in that blissful experience.

We also saw how the "I" that we keep thinking or saying is just a reference to the body, mind, intellect, or the roles that we play. The light of the real "I" is obscured by these false identities.

Since we now know that the entire story of the so-called "I" happens inside this body-mind, you may perhaps feel disillusioned. You might ponder, "What about everything I have tirelessly worked for? Everything I have accomplished, the challenges I have faced so far, and everything I have done for my family. If not me, then who did all that?"

The root cause of this disillusionment is our excessive attachment to our body-mind. We assume that our body, the roles we play, and the world around us constitute the totality of our existence. We forget our real identity and start believing in this illusion.

If someone mistakes a rope for a snake, they might get frightened and overwhelmed with thoughts like, "This is dangerous; I might die; everything will be over," and so on. Consequently, they may experience various sensations like rapid heartbeats and sweating, and visualize adverse outcomes.

Likewise, mistaking the material world to be the only truth, we get entangled in satiating the sensory cravings. For example, our eyes crave captivating sights; our ears desire soulful music; our taste buds long for delicious flavors; our skin craves soothing sensations; our nose desires pleasant aromas.

Moreover, we assume various roles in the world due to which we start suffering all the stress and expectations associated with them. We measure success and failure using societal standards. Attaining worldly success becomes our sole goal. However, living this way only causes worry and sorrow.

The mind has a habit of incessantly entertaining desires and chasing after them. As a result, it engages in comparisons and judgments. It judges and labels everything as good or bad, superior or inferior, dark or white, heavy or light. In every situation, it constantly chatters like a parrot, entangling us in its thoughts and emotions. We fall prey to the antics of this mind; whatever happens to the mind seems to happen to us. Consequently, we lose our peace.

Let's understand how the mind engages us in its comparison and judgment with an example.

There were two friends, both working in the same firm and drawing almost the same salary. Both received the same salary hike at the end of the company's performance appraisal cycle.

The first one thought, "Wow, this is great. Now I can try to better my life. My financial situation will improve."

The second one thought, "Oh, I received such a paltry salary rise. How will such a meager change benefit me? Prices of everything are skyrocketing each passing day!"

So, the salary hike being the same, it is the chatter of the mind that caused different reactions from both. The first friend was overjoyed while the other felt disappointed.

Since we identify ourselves with the mind, we believe in its chatter and experience joy and sorrow based on its reactions to events. With any incident, it is the thoughts that arise later and the incessant chatter of our judgmental mind that causes sorrow.

 Share a recent incident in which your mind caused disappointment due to its judgments and comparisons.

Whenever you get caught up in negative thoughts or emotions, carefully witness your thoughts to determine the truth.

The more you engage in observing your thoughts, the more you will understand how the illusion overpowers you. It may require patience and take time, but as your understanding deepens, you will confidently affirm, "This is merely an illusion, not the reality."

Until our next session, continue your practice of observing your thoughts and witness how you get caught up in the play of the mind. Thank you!

25

A Meditation to Culminate Our Journey

 This marks our final session. As we conclude, take a moment to reflect on the insights you have gained thus far. Jot down your thoughts.

You would have observed your body-mind playing different roles in your story. Could you witness how your body-mind becomes overwhelmed by various tendencies and character traits? When you observed your emotions and thoughts, did you find them lingering or gradually reducing in their intensity?

Regardless of your current state, as you mature in the practice of self-observation meditation and begin to comprehend the inner workings of your mind, the grip of your emotions will begin to weaken.

Whenever you have faced challenges, you may have probably resorted to temporary pleasures to escape them. However, these pleasures could only provide relief from your emotions for a while. Eventually, the same thoughts, troubles, and worries from the past and future would resurface.

Now, let's learn yet another meditation technique to strengthen the mind further, wherein the mind will become fully receptive and act on the new understanding received. This will help dissolve all the thoughts about the past and future accumulated in your mind, allowing you to live happily with true freedom. This meditation will help you transcend despair, embrace life with renewed hope, and distance yourself from all negative thoughts.

Liberation from past-future meditation

Please read the instructions first before practicing the meditation.

1. Sit in a comfortable posture. Set a timer of at least 15 minutes.
2. Close your eyes.
3. Take a moment to observe your body. If you feel any stress, stiffness, or exhaustion in any part, take a few deep breaths, relax that part, and settle your mind.
4. As you close your eyes, thoughts naturally arise. Initially, these thoughts may pertain to your daily activities, recent past, or immediate future. Just observe them without reacting to them. Gradually, your mind will calm down, and the frequency of thoughts will reduce.
5. Mentally affirm to yourself, "I have nothing to do, neither today nor tomorrow nor the day after."
6. When the mind tries to engage with some thoughts, gently bring a smile to your face and remind yourself, "Right now, the past or future does not exist, except in these thoughts. This is just a game of the mind. This beautiful lively moment of the present alone is the truth." Observe the thoughts as they pass.
7. When thoughts about the past and future trigger hurtful feelings, remind yourself, "The past does not bind me, nor am I trapped in the future. Everything exists here and now."

   This serves as a remedy for agony, and distracting thoughts will begin to dissolve. Express gratitude for all the past incidents, situations, emotions, thoughts, words, and actions that have evoked hurt and disappointment, as they now serve merely as a mirror in your body to remind you of your true nature beyond the body.
8. Finally, tell yourself, "May this understanding stay with me forever, allowing me to consciously play the role of a character and perceive all incidents in life with detachment."

9. Be immersed in the feeling of gratitude and open your eyes when the timer goes off.

Practicing this meditation regularly will strengthen your conviction that you are not the body; you are using this body as an instrument to play various roles in the world, but you are none of them. With this understanding, you will remain detached from the incidents that would previously upset you, ultimately freeing you from the grip of depression.

So far, we have explored many techniques to overcome depression and have also practiced some simple meditations. With these practices, you would have already experienced glimpses of freedom from depression. It is important to understand that depression is not an "incurable disease"; rather, it aggravates due to the suppression of feelings of despair over time. These feelings are a natural part of life. Instead of considering them as depression, view them as stepping stones toward growth. They can help us appreciate the feeling of happiness better.

As we conclude this counseling journey today, we have learned a new art of living a wonderful, stress-free life. While this knowledge has been imparted in a simple language, it is powerful and invaluable. Apply it to everyday incidents, no matter how trivial, to easily overcome depression and steer your life in a new direction. Also, guide others to follow this path of self-counselling.

The profound understanding and measures outlined in this book will elevate your life to such heights that you will experience lasting happiness and progress toward your ultimate goal. Do invest your time in contemplating the wisdom.

Our best wishes accompany you as you embark on this new journey. Thank you!

Appendix 1
Symptoms of Depression

So far, we have delved into the various aspects of depression, shedding light on its underlying causes, and techniques and meditations to overcome it. Now, we will gain a better understanding of the symptoms associated with depression.

In nature, everything undergoes change at every moment, whether it is an object, a living being, an animal, a bird, a plant, a microorganism, or inert matter. Whether visible or invisible, change is inherent and essential for development. The human body is no exception; it also undergoes constant changes. Development is an inherent process within the human body, mind, and brain.

While changes happening in the body may be partially visible or apparent, changes in feelings and thoughts are not physically visible. But they also undergo changes that contribute to development.

Trees, plants, the environment, weather, and climate change with time. However, except for humans, all other beings naturally adapt to these changes. Even a slight change can upset humans as their feelings and thoughts change every moment.

Thus, change is essential to leading a normal life. However, when our feelings and thoughts tend to become more negative than positive and start dominating us, it becomes a matter of concern.

When one is always engrossed in negative thoughts, one always seems to be upset. In such a state, one either spurts anger at someone or remains absorbed in despair and sorrow. Such behavior, when repeated, may make other people wonder if the person could be depressed.

While each person has different feelings and thoughts, there are some common symptoms among people with depression. Let's understand these symptoms better:

Physical symptoms

This refers to repeated physical pain or discomfort that appears to have no specific underlying cause, or which cannot be determined even after a medical investigation. For example,

- Frequent headaches, muscle tension, or body aches.
- Digestive issues, such as changes in appetite, nausea, indigestion, constipation, or diarrhea. Some may notice a decrease in appetite and subsequent weight loss, while some may have an increased appetite and weight gain.
- Sleep disturbances like insomnia where the person finds it difficult to fall asleep or stay asleep throughout the night. Others may experience excessive sleepiness and struggle to stay awake during the day.
- Fatigue or low energy levels despite getting enough rest.
- Dizziness, shortness of breath, etc.

Mental symptoms

Individuals with depression often experience persistent negative emotions and a generally low mood, with a few or all of the symptoms below.

- Emotional numbness or apathy in the form of a lack of interest, motivation, or responsiveness. Those experiencing apathy may appear indifferent, aloof, or unresponsive to their surroundings. Additionally, they may have a diminished capacity to experience and express emotions, which can result in a loss of will or drive they once had.

- A loss of interest or pleasure in previously enjoyed activities, hobbies, or social interactions.
- Difficulty in concentrating, making decisions, or experiencing memory problems.
- Persistent negative thoughts about themselves, feeling unworthy, guilty, or excessively self-critical.
- Anxiety or restlessness may coexist with depression in some instances.
- Suicidal thoughts or tendencies can occur in severe cases of depression, requiring immediate professional intervention.

Social symptoms

The specific manifestation of social symptoms can depend on various factors, including an individual's personality, past experiences, coping mechanisms, and the severity of their depression.

- Distancing from family, friends, and social interactions. Tendency to isolate themselves and withdraw from social events or gatherings. Some individuals may actively seek attention or support for their condition, expressing their struggles openly.
- Experience difficulty in initiating or maintaining conversations. They find it challenging to engage with others or express themselves.
- Feelings of insecurity or inferiority may arise, leading to comparisons with others and harboring resentment toward others' perceived well-being.
- Diminishing interest in activities or events previously enjoyed.
- Depression can sometimes be accompanied by fear or anxiety related to specific things or situations (phobias). This can manifest as avoidance of particular places, activities, or experiences.

Symptoms related to finance management

The impact of socioeconomic factors on mental health should not be overlooked, as financial difficulties can contribute to developing depressive symptoms. Hence, it is vital to acknowledge the complex interplay between depression and socioeconomic status.

It is essential to consider the individual circumstances and factors contributing to financial challenges and the potential impact of depression on financial decision-making. For some individuals, financial constraints or losses can serve as potential triggers for their depression.

Individuals with depression may exhibit changes in their attitudes and behaviors toward financial matters. However, these changes are not universal and can vary from person to person.

Some may struggle with managing their finances, job, or business issues or lack attention or motivation toward financial responsibilities.

Depression can significantly impact various areas of an individual's life, but it is not true that every depressed person will exhibit all the characteristics mentioned above. These characteristics represent possibilities and can vary among individuals and situations. If some of these characteristics are prevalent and pronounced, the individual or their acquaintances must be alert and seek appropriate treatment.

Early intervention and seeking help from a healthcare professional are beneficial in managing depression. However, it is crucial to understand that overcoming depression is a multifaceted process that may require a combination of treatments and support. Recovery experiences can vary, and personalized care is essential for everyone.

Appendix 2
Guidelines for Caregivers

People often have questions about the extent to which they should advise, support, and pay attention to individuals who are depressed. Although there is no precise and definitive answer, some guidance is provided.

Let's consider the story of Kiran, a young girl from Kanpur, India, living with her parents. She was very cheerful, vibrant, and mature beyond her age. She always had a smile on her face. She had a strong bond with her father, whom she looked up to as her hero.

Of late, she noticed a change in her father's behavior. He started keeping quiet and seemed lost in his thoughts. He would come home from work and go straight to his room without saying a word. Kiran found this strange as he was otherwise very talkative and loved spending time with the family.

She felt concerned for him and tried to talk to him. However, whenever she tried to bring up the topic, he shifted the conversation to another topic. Kiran didn't know what to do.

One day, she discussed the issue with her friend Rita. Rita told her that keeping quiet and avoiding conversations could be signs of depression. Kiran was shocked to know this. She realized that her father might be going through a rough patch and needed help.

Kiran persevered in her efforts to understand her father. Although he was initially hesitant to speak, he eventually opened up to her. She actively listened to him, observed his behavior and mood, and empathetically tried to see things from his perspective.

Through this process, she gradually discovered that her father was experiencing sadness due to unfulfilled dreams that he believed were unattainable, given his other responsibilities.

Recognizing that her father's depression stemmed from unfulfilled aspirations, Kiran understood that a quick fix would not suffice. Instead, she provided unwavering support and encouragement, acknowledging the challenges he faced. Together, they explored alternative possibilities and identified realistic steps toward realizing his dreams. This ongoing process required patience and understanding.

It is important to note that this example simplifies a complex situation, and each person's experience with depression is unique. While Kiran's approach proved beneficial for her father, it may not apply to every individual with depression. The causes, severity, and solutions for depression can vary greatly.

For instance, some individuals find solace in food, while others do not. Some appreciate the attention they receive, while others prefer more distance. Therefore, addressing depression often requires a combination of approaches, including therapy, medication, lifestyle changes, and a supportive network of family and friends. Sensitivity, empathy, and guidance are crucial when dealing with depression to ensure the best possible outcomes for those affected. Every person's attitude and desires differ.

When we understand what the other person wishes, their preferred topics, and how they respond to certain words, we can determine what to say and avoid. Engaging in diverse conversations, asking questions, and actively listening allows them to express themselves freely.

When we genuinely comprehend and address their perspective, they build trust in us. Consequently, they become more receptive to listening and understanding us.

Additionally, when dealing with individuals suffering from depression, it is essential to consider the following:

- Assess the appropriate level of attention to provide and what aspects to overlook when assisting a person with depression. Avoid becoming overly absorbed in their despair, which may lead to constant worry and sadness.

- Encouraging self-reliance is crucial. While wholeheartedly assisting the person and attentively listening to them is essential, it is equally important to help them become independent. Sometimes, individuals become overly reliant on external support and expect others to solve all their problems. Setting boundaries and clarifying the extent of our assistance encourages them to take initiative. Consistent encouragement will boost confidence and aid recovery.

- Patience is vital when interacting with the person. Everyone has unique circumstances, personality traits, and issues. Some individuals with depression choose not to confide in anyone due to past experiences and a general distrust of others. Dealing with such individuals requires greater patience.

- It is not always necessary to assume they are wrong and constantly explain things to them. Many individuals with depression often become frustrated, saying, "Everyone tells me what I should do, but no one is willing to understand me." Consequently, they may withdraw from sharing their thoughts and emotions.

Each person's experience with depression is unique, and the reasons for their condition can vary significantly. It is important to acknowledge that when assisting individuals with depression, they may have different preferences and needs:

- Some individuals may feel abandoned if we begin helping them but maintain emotional barriers or abruptly withdraw support. This abandonment can worsen their condition and lead to a downward spiral. In such cases, providing consistent and reliable support is crucial, ensuring they feel cared for and not left alone in their struggle.

- On the other hand, some individuals may prefer a certain distance, keeping others at arm's length. They may feel overwhelmed or uncomfortable with excessive closeness or intrusion into their personal space. Respecting their boundaries and providing support while respecting their need for freedom can foster trust and allow them to navigate their journey at their own pace.

When supporting someone with depression, giving wholehearted effort and attention is essential. Providing help without genuine dedication or maintaining emotional barriers can create false hope or a sense of abandonment. In such cases, it may be better to avoid offering assistance altogether. Insufficient support can aggravate their feelings of hopelessness and increase the risk of self-harm, leading to guilt and regret for not giving their best efforts.

Therefore, it is crucial to approach supporting someone with depression with sincerity, empathy, and a commitment to being available for them. By fully investing our time, energy, and emotional support, we can foster trust, provide a lifeline during their darkest moments, and significantly impact their journey toward healing.

However, it is essential to remember that we cannot shoulder the sole responsibility for someone else's mental health. Depression is a complex issue that often requires professional intervention. If we feel overwhelmed or unsure about the level of support we can provide, seeking guidance from mental health professionals who can offer appropriate strategies and resources is essential.

Lastly, it is essential to maintain inner peace and avoid fixating on immediate outcomes. Instant results should not be expected, and if the person is unresponsive, different approaches can be explored.

By experimenting with varied approaches persistently, we may discover that our commitment and unwavering faith yield positive results, gradually helping the individual overcome their depression.

Appendix 3
Singing Therapy

Do you appreciate the importance of music?

Even if one has everything in life, it seems incomplete without music.

Life is a song of love that everyone must sing. The melody of music brings rhythm and harmony to our life. For this, we should keep humming songs.

Oh! Don't be afraid. You do not have to sing any difficult songs. Just list the situations from your life along with the techniques you have learned in this book in the form of a song and sing when thoughts of despair trouble you or you feel scared of something. Just as slow and harmonious melodies are always helpful in soothing the mind, such singing will give solace in times of distress.

Make use of these phrases in your song - "It doesn't matter; it's not a big deal; it's just a matter of…; even this will pass away; bother then when 'then' becomes now." There is a deep understanding hidden in these lines. They can help calm your mind. Hence, hum them when you feel despair or discomfort.

Considering commonplace situations, some examples are given here.

For example, suppose a housewife is worrying about preparing a big feast for the guests arriving after 2 to 3 days, she can sing as follows:

The servants are on leave. It doesn't matter.

No groceries and veggies. It's not a big deal.

Cooking for so many. It's not a big deal.

Will guests enjoy it? Bother then when 'then' becomes now.

When will the guests leave? It's just a matter of time.

I've been toiling hard for so long. Even this will pass away.

Consider another example of someone who is stressed due to challenges at the workplace. They can adopt the same phrases to address their context as follows.

A colleague got a raise. It doesn't matter.

I wasn't praised. It's not a big deal.

Will I be relocated? Bother then when 'then' becomes now.

When will I get a holiday? It's just a matter of a few days.

When will this ordeal end? Even this will pass away.

Someone suffering from a financial crisis can sing the lines as follows.

How can I settle my bills? It's not a big deal.

Job search in vain. It's just a matter of a few days.

Interest rates are on the rise. It doesn't matter.

Will I need to sell my house? Bother then when 'then' becomes now.

I'm burdened with this loan. Even this will pass away.

Someone suffering from physical ailments can sing the lines as follows.

How long will I be sick? It's just a matter of a few days.

Will it aggravate into a major illness? It's not a big deal.

Will I be shifted to ICU? It doesn't matter.

How will I pay these hefty bills? Bother then when 'then' becomes now.

I'm fed up being sick. Even this will pass away.

A student can sing the lines as follows.

How will I cope with the tough syllabus? It's not a big deal.

Will I get a good job? Bother then when 'then' becomes now.

My classmates are getting better placements. It doesn't matter.

When will I get a break from my studies? Even this will pass away.

In this way, you can express your problems in the form of a song and sing them. You don't have to be a good singer for this. This is an easy way to escape your despair and become free from grief and anxiety.

Let's end this session here. May happiness spread new colors in your life. Take pleasure in all the colors nature has to offer.

Thank you, wish you the best!

Appendix 4
Understanding Depression and its Causes: A Statistical Summary

1. Global Impact: According to the World Health Organization (WHO), depression is the leading cause of disability worldwide, with an estimated disability weight of 3.2% [WHO depression statistics]. This means it contributes significantly to years lived with disability (YLDs).

2. Global Increase: Due to the COVID-19 pandemic, the WHO reports a 25% increase in the prevalence of anxiety and depression globally, with an estimated additional 76 million cases in the first year of the pandemic alone [WHO pandemic and mental health].

3. Total Affected: The WHO estimates roughly 280 million people globally have depression (as of 2020) [WHO depression statistics]. That translates to roughly 1 in 7 people worldwide.

4. Gender Disparity: Women are diagnosed with depression about 50% more often than men, according to the WHO. This translates to roughly 5.5% of adult women and 3.7% of adult men globally experiencing depression [WHO depression statistics].

5. Perinatal Depression: Affecting 10%-15% of pregnant women and new mothers, perinatal depression is a significant concern, according to the National Institute of Mental Health (NIMH). That translates to roughly 600,000 women experiencing perinatal depression in the US each year [NIMH perinatal depression].

6. Adolescent Rates: According to the NIMH, 16.6% of adolescents in the US experience a major depressive episode in a given year. That translates to roughly 3.2 million adolescents (aged 12-17) experiencing depression annually [NIMH depression statistics].

7. Racial and Ethnic Disparities: According to a recent Gallup poll, lifetime depression rates are rising fastest among Black and Hispanic adults in the US, with 20.6% and 18.3% reporting a diagnosis respectively [Gallup depression rates].

8. Comorbidity: According to the Depression and Bipolar Support Alliance, depression often co-occurs with other medical conditions. For example, people with depression are 59% more likely to have an adverse cardiovascular event and 25% of cancer patients experience depression [DBS Alliance depression statistics].

9. Suicide Risk: Major depression is a significant risk factor for suicide, the fourth leading cause of death among 15 to 29 year olds, according to the WHO. Over 700,000 people die by suicide every year globally, and depression is a major contributing factor [WHO depression statistics].

10. US Prevalence: The National Institute of Mental Health (NIMH) reports that an estimated 21 million adults in the US experienced major depression in 2021. This represents 8.4% of US adults [NIMH depression statistics].

11. US Prevalence by Age: According to the NIMH, young adults (aged 18-25) have the highest prevalence of major depressive episodes in the US at 18.6%. This means nearly 1 in 5 young adults experience depression [NIMH depression statistics].

12. Economic Impact: According to the National Alliance on Mental Illness (NAMI), depression costs the US economy an estimated $210.5 billion per year in lost productivity and medical expenses [NAMI depression statistics].

13. Untreated Depression: The WHO reports that globally, over half (59%) of those with depression do not receive treatment [WHO depression statistics]. There are many reasons for this, including stigma and lack of access to healthcare.

14. Stigma: According to NAMI, stigma surrounding mental health conditions like depression can prevent people from seeking help. Roughly two-thirds of adults in the US report feeling some level of stigma around mental illness [NAMI depression stigma].

15. Meditation's Impact on the Brain: Research suggests meditation may have positive effects on brain regions involved in mood regulation. A 2017 study in Psychiatry Research: Neuroimaging found that after an eight-week meditation program, participants with depression showed increased gray matter volume in the hippocampus, a part of the brain important for learning and mood regulation [Brain imaging study on meditation].

16. Social Connection: Social isolation can worsen depression. Strong social connections can provide a sense of belonging and support, which can be protective against depression, according to the National Alliance on Mental Illness (NAMI) [NAMI social support and mental health].

17. Mindfulness-Based Cognitive Therapy (MBCT): This well-established frontrunner combines mindfulness meditation with CBT techniques. A 2016 study published in JAMA Internal Medicine found MBCT to be as effective as medication (an SSRI) in preventing relapse of depression in adults with a history of major depressive episodes [JAMA study on MBCT].

18. A large body of research supports this concept. A good starting point is a review by Keng et al. (2011) published in Clinical Psychology Review titled "Mindfulness training for psychological wellbeing: A meta-analysis of randomized controlled trials." This review analyzes findings from numerous studies and highlights

the positive effects of mindfulness meditation on reducing stress and improving emotional regulation.

19. Mindfulness Meditation-Based Pain Relief: A Mechanistic Account published in the Annals of the New York Academy of Sciences in 2016. This study explored the mechanisms underlying the pain-relieving effects of mindfulness meditation.

20. Sharper Focus and Emotional Control: A 2020 study published in Brain and Cognition found that mindfulness meditation training can sharpen cognitive control and reduce emotional reactivity in healthy adults. This means meditation can help you focus better and manage your emotions more effectively.

21. A recent 2022 multi-center study published in Frontiers in Psychology showed that a mindfulness meditation program significantly reduced work-related stress and burnout symptoms among employees. This suggests that meditation can be a powerful tool for improving well-being in the workplace.

22. Brain Changes with Mindfulness: A 2020 review in Neuroscience and Biobehavioral Reviews analyzed brain imaging studies. The review found evidence that mindfulness-based interventions for depression led to changes in brain regions linked to mood regulation. This suggests that meditation may positively impact the brains of individuals with depression.

23. Mindfulness for Treatment-Resistant Depression: A 2023 review in the American Journal of Psychotherapy explored the use of mindfulness-based interventions (including meditation) for treatment-resistant depression.

24. Mindfulness and Self-Esteem: A 2021 study in Frontiers in Psychology found that mindfulness meditation practices were associated with increased self-esteem in individuals with depression. According to the researchers, this boost in self-esteem

may contribute to the overall positive effects of mindfulness on depression symptoms.

25. Long-Term Benefits of Mindfulness: According to a 2018 study in Depression and Anxiety, the positive effects of mindfulness-based interventions for depression can be sustained over time. This suggests that consistent mindfulness practice can offer long-term benefits for managing depression.

Depression is a complex mental health condition, and its causes can vary from person to person. It is generally believed that a combination of genetic, biological, environmental, and psychological factors contributes to the development of depression. Here are some of the leading causes and risk factors associated with depression:

1. Genetics: Evidence suggests that a family history of depression or other mood disorders can increase an individual's susceptibility to developing depression. Certain genetic variations may make some individuals more vulnerable to the condition.

2. Brain chemistry and biology: Imbalances in certain neurotransmitters, such as serotonin, norepinephrine, and dopamine, which are involved in regulating mood, can play a role in the development of depression. Additionally, changes in the structure or function of the brain, particularly in areas related to mood regulation and emotional processing, have been observed in people with depression.

3. Environmental factors: Various environmental factors can contribute to depression, including:

    - Stressful life events: Traumatic experiences, such as losing a loved one, relationship problems, financial difficulties, or other significant life changes, can trigger or exacerbate depression.

- Childhood trauma: Experiencing neglect, abuse, or other adverse childhood experiences can increase the risk of developing depression later in life.
- Chronic illness: Certain medical conditions, such as chronic pain, cancer, diabetes, or heart disease, can contribute to depression.
- Substance abuse: Drug or alcohol abuse can cause and be a consequence of depression. Substance abuse can worsen depressive symptoms and make it harder to recover.

4. Psychological factors: Certain personality traits and psychological factors may increase the risk of depression, including:
    - Low self-esteem or negative self-image
    - Pessimistic thinking or a tendency to ruminate on negative thoughts
    - History of anxiety or other mental health disorders
    - Difficulty coping with stress or adapting to changes
    - A perfectionistic or self-critical mindset

It is important to note that depression is a multifaceted condition, and not everyone with depression will have the same causes or risk factors. Each individual's experience with depression is unique, and it often involves a combination of multiple factors interacting with each other.

References for Statistics

1. World Health Organization. (2020). Depression. https://www.who.int/news-room/fact-sheets/detail/depression
2. World Health Organization. (2020). COVID-19 pandemic triggers 25% increase in prevalence of anxiety and depression in first year https://www.who.int/teams/mental-health-and-substance-use/mental-health-and-covid-19

3. Newport, F. (2023, January 12). Lifetime Diagnosis of Depression Rises Among Blacks and Hispanics. Gallup. https://sprc.org/news/u-s-depression-rates-reach-new-highs/

4. Depression and Bipolar Support Alliance. (2019). Depression Statistics. https://www.dbsalliance.org/education/depression/

5. World Health Organization. (2019). Suicide. https://www.who.int/data/gho/data/themes/mental-health/suicide-rates

6. National Institute of Mental Health. (2022). Major Depressive Episode. https://www.nimh.nih.gov/health/statistics/major-depression

7. National Alliance on Mental Illness. (2015). The Economic Impact of Mental Illness. https://www.nami.org/Extranet/NAMI-State-Organization-and-NAMI-Affiliate-Leaders/NAMI-State-Organization-and-NAMI-Affiliate-Leaders/Financial-and-Risk-Management/2021-NAMI-Impact-Report_11-19-compress

8. World Health Organization. (2020). Depression. https://www.who.int/news-room/fact-sheets/detail/depression

9. National Alliance on Mental Illness. (2019). Stigma. https://www.nami.org/Get-Involved/Pledge-to-Be-StigmaFree

10. Lazar, S. W., Kerr, C. E., Williams, R. L., & Benson, H. (2015). Meditation experience is associated with increased cortical thickness. Social Cognitive and Affective Neuroscience, 10(8), 1007-1014. https://www.ncbi.nlm.nih.gov/pmc/articles/PMC1361002/

11. National Alliance on Mental Illness. (2019). Mental Health Conditions and Social Support. https://www.nami.org/Home

12. Keng, N., Siu, A., & Phillips, K. (2011). Mindfulness training for psychological wellbeing: A meta-analysis of randomized controlled trials. Clinical Psychology Review, 31(6), 701-716. https://psycnet.apa.org/record/2021-39074-014

13. Segal, Z. V., Williams, J. M. W., & Teasdale, J. D. (2016). Mindfulness-based cognitive therapy for depression: A meta-analysis

of the anti-relapse effect. JAMA Internal Medicine, 176(7), 1006-1011. https://pubmed.ncbi.nlm.nih.gov/21802618/

14. Keng, N., Siu, A., & Phillips, K. (2011). Mindfulness training for psychological wellbeing: A meta-analysis of randomized controlled trials. Clinical Psychology Review, 31(6), 701-716.

Appendix 5
Revision Chart

No.	How are you feeling?	How to act on it
1	Feeling caught up in injured memories or traumas of the past	Visualize the incident in fast-forward mode like a comedy scene with cartoon characters and voices. (Session 1)
2	Feeling a diminished desire to live	Refer and apply the 3H solution and read inspiring biographies. (Session 5)
3	Feeling upset or dejected	Recall positive or happy events of the past (Session 5)
4	Feeling hatred and self-loathing	Embrace yourself and tell yourself "I love you as you are." (Session 6)
5	Overwhelmed with negative feelings about the present	Repeat the mantra, "Even this will pass away." (Session 7)
6	Feeling impatient and restless	Remember the tortoise. Apply the Outlook and Overlook techniques (Session 8)
7	Feeling upset	Repeat the mantra, "It's just a matter of ___." (Session 9)
8	Caught up in excessive thinking	Defocus from what has already happened and instead, focus and act on current possibilities (Session 10)
9	Feeling lonely	Take help of diet, exercises, and nature (Session 11)
10	Feeling bored or fed up	Shift your focus and engage in a creative endeavor. (Session 12)
11	Getting stuck in trivial matters	Repeat the mantra, "It doesn't matter." (Session 13)

No.	How are you feeling?	How to act on it
12	Feeling troubled about the present situation	Repeat the mantra, "It's not a big deal." (Session 14)
13	Worried about the future	"Bother then, when 'then' becomes now." (Session 17)
14	Feeling hurt in relationships	Ask yourself, "How long do I choose to remain in this hurtful state?" (Session 18)
15	Feeling dullness and lethargy	Witness your emotions and say "Next" to every thought that arises (Session 19)
16	Feeling hopeless and losing faith	Keep faith and repeat the Voice of Faith affirmations (Session 22)
17	Feeling troubled about the happenings in life	Witness life as the story of a character in the drama of life (Session 23)
18	Imbalance in thoughts	Practice the meditation to heal the distress of the past (Session 15), and the meditation for liberation from past-future (Session 25)
19	When others appear depressed	Listen to them with detachment, patience and empathy. (Appendix 2)
20	Feeling despair or melancholy	Sing by applying the mantras to your situation (Appendix 3)

• • •

You can mail your opinion or feedback on this book to:
books.feedback@tejgyan.org

About Sirshree

Sirshree's spiritual quest, which began during his childhood, led him on a journey through various schools of philosophy and meditation practices. He studied a wide range of literature on mind science and spirituality. After a long period of deep contemplation on the truth of life, his quest culminated in attaining the ultimate truth.

Sirshree espouses, "All spiritual paths that lead to the truth begin differently but culminate at the same point – Understanding. This understanding is complete in itself. Listening to this understanding is enough to attain the Truth." Over the last two decades, he has dedicated his life to raise mass consciousness.

Sirshree has delivered more than 4000 discourses that throw light on this understanding. He has designed a system for wisdom, which makes it accessible to all. This system has inspired people from all walks of life to progress on their journey of the Truth. Thousands of seekers join in a virtual prayer for World Peace and Global Healing daily at 9:09 am and 9:09 pm.

About Tej Gyan Foundation

Tej Gyan Foundation is a non-profit organization founded on the teachings of Sirshree. The Foundation disseminates Tejgyan – the wisdom that guides one from self-development to Self-realization, leading towards Self-stabilization.

The Foundation's system for imparting wisdom has been assessed by international quality auditors and accredited with the ISO 9001:2015 certification. This wisdom has been presented in a simple, systematic, and practically applicable form that makes it accessible to people from all walks of life, regardless of religion, caste, social strata, country, or belief system.

The Foundation has centers in more than 400 cities and towns across India and other countries. The mission of Tej Gyan Foundation is to create a highly evolved society by leading seekers from negative thoughts to positive thoughts and further, from positive thoughts to Happy thoughts. A 'Happy thought' is the auspicious thought of being free from all thoughts, leading to the state of supreme bliss beyond thoughts.

If you seek such wisdom that leads you beyond mere knowledge, dissolves all problems, frees you from all limiting beliefs, reveals the true nature of divinity, and establishes you in the ultimate truth, then it is time to discover Tejgyan; it is time to rise above the mundane knowledge of words and experience Tejgyan!

The MahaAasmani Magic of Awakening Retreat

Self-development to Self-realization towards Self-stabilization

Do you wish to experience unconditional happiness that is not dependent on any reason? Happiness that is permanent and only increases with time? Do you wish to experience love, peace, self-belief, harmony in relationships, prosperity, and true contentment? Do you wish to progress in all facets of your life, viz. physical, mental, social, financial, and spiritual?

If you seek answers to these questions and are thirsty for the ultimate truth, then you are welcome to participate in the MahaAasmani Magic of Awakening retreat organized by Tej Gyan Foundation. This is the Foundation's flagship retreat based on the teachings of Sirshree.

The purpose of this retreat

The purpose of this retreat is that every human being should:

- Discover the answer to "Who am I" and "Why am I?" through direct experience and be established in ultimate bliss.

- Learn the art of living in the present, free from the burden of the past and the anxiety of the future.

- Acquire practical tools to help quieten the chattering mind and dissolve problems.

- Discover missing links in the practices of Meditation (*Dhyana*), Action (*Karma*), Wisdom (*Gyana*), and Devotion (*Bhakti*).

About Books by Sirshree

Sirshree's published work includes more than 150 book titles, some of which have been translated into more than 10 languages. His literature provides a profound reading on various topics of practical living and unravels the missing links in karma, wisdom, devotion, meditation, and consciousness.

His books have been published by leading publishing houses like Penguin, Hay House, Bloomsbury, Wisdom Tree, Jaico, etc. "The Source" book series, authored by Sirshree, has sold over 10 million copies. Various luminaries and celebrities like His Holiness the Dalai Lama, publishers Mr. Reid Tracy, Ms. Tami Simon and Yoga Master Dr. B. K. S. Iyengar have released Sirshree's books and lauded his work.

The Source
Attain Both, Inner Peace
and Worldly success

Awaken the Power of Faith
Discover the 7 Principles of the
Highest Power of the Universe

To order books authored by Sirshree, login to:
www.gethappythoughts.org
For further details, call: +91 9011013210

SELECT BOOKS AUTHORED BY SIRSHREE

   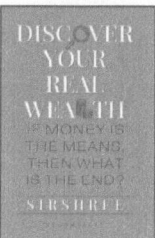

To order these and other books authored by Sirshree
Visit **www.gethappythoughts.org**

Tej Gyan Foundation – Contact details

Registered Office:
Happy Thoughts Building, Vikrant Complex, Near Tapovan Mandir, Pimpri, Pune 411017, INDIA. Contact: +91 20-27411240, +91 20-27412576

MaNaN Ashram:
Survey No. 43, Sanas Nagar, Nandoshi Gaon, Kirkatwadi Phata, Off Sinhagad Road, Taluka Haveli, Pune district - 411024, INDIA. Contact: +91 992100 8060.

WORLD PEACE PRAYER

Divine Light of Love, Bliss, and Peace is Showering;

The Golden Light of Higher Consciousness is Rising;

All negativity on Earth is Dissolving;

Everyone is in Peace and Blissfully Shining;

O God, Gratitude for Everything!

Members of Tej Gyan Foundation have been offering this impersonal mass prayer for many years. Those who are happy can offer this prayer. Those feeling low or suffering from illness can receive healing with this prayer.

If you are feeling troubled or sick, please sit to receive the healing effect of this prayer. Visualize that the divine white healing light is being showered on earth through the prayers of thousands and is also reaching you, bringing you peace and good health. You can dwell in this feeling for some time and then offer your gratitude to those offering the prayer.

A Humble Appeal

More than a million peace lovers pray for World Peace and Global Healing every morning and evening at 9:09. Also, a prayer (in Hindi) to elevate consciousness is webcast every day on YouTube at 3:30 pm and 9:00 pm IST. Please participate in this noble endeavor.

www.ingramcontent.com/pod-product-compliance
Lightning Source LLC
LaVergne TN
LVHW041842070526
838199LV00045BA/1406